HOW TO LIVE
IN THE
WOODS

Expert Advice on
Planning, Outfitting, & Managing
a Camping Expedition

Homer Halsted

Illustrated by
Don G. Kelley

Dover Publications, Inc.
Mineola, New York

Bibliographical Note

This Dover edition, first published in 2019, is an unabridged republication of *How to Live in the Woods: Here is Expert Advice on Planning, Outfitting, and Managing the Camping Expedition*, originally published in 1948 by Little, Brown and Company, Boston. Readers should be aware that the information in Chapter VI: "Where to Go," referring to the addresses of government conservation and wildlife departments is out of date and has been included for the sake of authenticity. Interested readers can easily obtain such information online or from a local government office.

Library of Congress Cataloging-in-Publication Data

Names: Halsted, Homer, author. | Kelley, Don G. (Don Graeme), illustrator.
Title: How to live in the woods : expert advice on planning, outfitting, and
    managing a camping expedition / Homer Halsted ; illustrated by Don G.
    Kelley.
Description: Mineola, New York : Dover Publications, Inc., 2019. | Includes
    index. | "This Dover edition, first published in 2019, is an unabridged
    republication of How to Live in the Woods: Here is Expert Advice on
    Planning, Outfitting, and Managing the Camping Expedition, originally
    published in 1948 by Little, Brown and Company, Boston. Readers should be
    aware that the information in Chapter VI: "Where to Go," referring to the
    addresses of government conservation and wildlife departments is out of
    date and no longer valid. It is included for the sake of authenticity to
    the original edition. Interested readers can easily obtain such information
    online or from a local government office"—Title page verso.
Identifiers: LCCN 2019007738 | ISBN 9780486836669 | ISBN 0486836665
Subjects: LCSH: Camping.
Classification: LCC GV191.7 .H344 2019 | DDC 796.54—dc23
LC record available at https://lccn.loc.gov/2019007738

Manufactured in the United States by LSC Communications
83666501   2019
www.doverpublications.com

FOREWORD

There is no apparent need for an elaborate introduction to this little book on camping. Better writers have long since portrayed all the joys of life in the open and I could add nothing in the way of inspiration.

Assuming that you already have the urge to seek recreation outdoors, I shall attempt to tell you how, rather than why, and hope for the best. You may take to the woods to dodge the sheriff or hunt buried treasure, for all I care; my interest is in your preparation for the excursion.

Sadly enough, most of us have inherited more pioneer spirit than pioneer skill and are too strongly inclined to the belief that Nature's bounty may be ours for the taking. We are apt to rush into the forest with lots of enthusiasm and little judgment, to return, sometimes, with sour recollections as principal souvenirs of our expeditions.

It is one thing to dream of pungent campfires beside sparkling waters and something else again to cook over them. It is pleasant enough to imagine yourself conquering the wilderness with little besides gun and ax, but most disillusioning to discover that bad weather and insects may neither be shot nor chopped down. Old Mother Nature is a catankerous hussy, at times, and works a lot of little jokers into the bargaining for her delights. The starry-eyed tenderfoot has little chance of besting her, without a few aces up his sleeve.

So far as I remember, the Swiss Family Robinsons were the only historical campers ever to be fully equipped by their biographer. The others appear to have set forth on their adventures with nothing much more than leather pants and rugged constitutions, evidently ordained to sleep on the soft sides of rocks and eat whatever they could tear loose from the fauna and flora. Maybe that was hot stuff, in those good old days, but if you try it, the result may be distress or big trouble with conservation officers.

There is no reason for the modern woodsman to make an endurance test of his occasional outing, or to devote a major share of his all-too-brief vacation to the business of providing decent comfort. He can, if he will, equip for fun and convenience, with things the old-timers never dreamed of, and gain a deal of enjoyment in the doing. I aim to outline the details, so far as my limitations permit.

CONTENTS

HOW TO LIVE

IN THE

WOODS

I

THE APPROACH TO CAMPING

Camp life, however brief, can put a strain on almost any human relationship. The effort required to maintain decent circumstances, the constant proximity of one or a few persons and the necessity of sharing conditions on equal terms will shortly uncover any faults of character which may be lying around loose. If such faults are major and many, the jolly companions may fall to quarreling and completely defeat the purpose of the outing.

Should you happen, sometime, to spend about three rainy days in close quarters with a whiner or a persistent shirker of duty, you'll soon discover the unpleasant side of human nature — probably your own. So, choose your companions most carefully and be certain that you, yourself, intend to be a good one.

If you can acquire some skill in cooking, woodcutting, bedmaking or dishwashing, popularity is fairly well assured, but in any case start out with the earnest intention of being willing to work, even if hopelessly awkward. The unhandiest person in the world can at least carry firewood, peel potatoes and bury garbage, without being coaxed or urged to do his share. He can also be cheerful and considerate of others; not only of their feelings, but of their equipment as well.

Most woodsmen are proud of their outfits and often jealous of them to boot. Avoid criticism of the other fellow's equipment and make sure he is agreeable before you appropriate any of it, even for a minute.

Take some pains, as you find time, to learn the means of overcoming your natural deficiencies.

City parks frequently afford opportunities for the practice of boating and canoeing; swimming lessons may be had in nearly any Y.M.C.A. and your neighbor's Boy Scout son can teach you a few simple knots. Learn to clean your own gun, unravel a fishing line, sharpen a knife or an ax and dry out a pair of boots. Actually, a great deal of such skill may be acquired before you ever set foot off pavement and it will add immeasurably to your fun and the respect of your companions.

Unless you boast too much, no one will expect you to be a veritable Nimrod, but your best friend will eventually tire of waiting on you and contributing his equipment and skill to your selfish enjoyment. Self-sufficiency affords more satisfaction to a camper than any other one thing. Practice up on it as you can.

II

GETTING READY TO GO

The camper's first concern is his footwear and clothing, which must provide protection from the elements in many varied circumstances. He will have to reckon with wind and rain, when "spares" are far away, and rocks and brush, which will tear the life out of any but the toughest apparel. There will be no neighborhood haberdashery in which to replenish his wardrobe if shoes or pants succumb to rough usage, and his pack must supply his needs, come what may.

So, it behooves him to outfit with careful consideration for the job in hand; figuring to go light, as proof of self-sufficiency, but right, for the sake of comfort and decency. A compact and efficient kit of well-chosen items will afford far greater satisfaction than a trunkful of odds and ends.

Personal equipment, other than wearing apparel, is also of great importance. The bathroom shelf will be far behind when you arrive in camp, and the toothbrush at home will clean no teeth in the woods. Nor will the druggist be within call, to administer a physic on demand.

Some provision must be made for maintenance and repair. The most humble item of equipment becomes precious when you need it and have no substitute, and so deserves to be kept in serviceable condition. To that end, clothes must be mended, cutlery sharpened and guns cleaned, as occasion arises. You should not depend upon others to supply the means.

Your companions will expect you to show up with sufficient equipment to provide for your own comfort and convenience and will mark you down as a "shiftless skunk" if you don't.

A complete list of the necessities appears something like this:

    Suitable clothing and footwear
    Spare clothing (underwear, socks, sweater, etc.)
    Raincoat
    Slippers or moccasins (for a change)
    Pocket equipment (knife, compass, matchsafe, etc.)
    Toilet kit (including soap and towels)
    First-aid kit
    Mending kit (needles, thread, buttons, etc.)
    Flashlight
    Matches
    Tobacco

And such seasonal or special equipment as:

    Gun-cleaning kit
    Reel oil
    Bug dope
    Sun glasses
    Boot grease, etc.

I'll elaborate on most of these items as I go along.

Apparel

UNDERWEAR for outdoor use in any but hot weather should be wool or part wool. Even in summer, wool serves to ward off chills after the body has become wet from perspiration or rain. You will vary the weight of the garments in accordance with the season, of course. Drawers should have full or three-quarter-length legs, to foil the bugs which get up your pants legs, and shirts may well have long sleeves for protection of arms and wrists. Separate shirts and drawers are superior to union suits, as they are easier to change after a partial ducking and far handier to wash.

SOCKS should be of soft, heavy wool; the best quality you can afford, and perfectly fitted. Your tender feet will need such protection from excess perspiration and rough trails, when on the march.

BOOTS merit the most particular attention, as poor ones can easily ruin any trip. For most seasons of the year, soft leather boots made in moccasin style, but with flexible composition soles and rubber heels, are very satisfactory. Regular moccasins, with no soles or heels, are pretty harsh on city feet if much walking is to be done, but are fine for wear around camp or in a canoe. The high-top boot of the Army stores and the mail-order catalogues is of little value to a woodsman. It weighs too much; has stiff, heavy soles; cramps the leg muscles; prevents proper ventilation of the feet and requires too much time for putting on and taking off. The high tops serve no purpose other than confining the bottoms of breeches legs, which long socks would do as well. The same long socks, inside loose trouser legs, would probably defeat snake fangs to better effect than tight leather boot tops. No boot top is ever high enough to prevent going in over where water is encountered.

I like a 9-inch "bird shooter" style boot better than any other, for all-round use. The tops are high enough to keep out pebbles and sticks kicked up in walking and serve to confine the bottoms of trouser legs when occasion demands. There are no hooks to catch grass and brush. The composition soles hold well on rock, dry grass and pine needles and are beautifully flexible for walking. They wear wonderfully well and afford good footing on logs.

For wet going, in snow or marsh, rubber boots are needed. There are many styles, ranging from the common hip boot to leather-top rubbers, the favorite of most woodsmen. These are heavier than leather boots and unsuitable for mild weather hiking, as they condense and hold perspiration. They are treacherous on wet logs and ice, especially after the soles are worn smooth, but you may wear ice creepers with them to good effect.

You should use a good boot grease or dubbing on leather boots, applying it often and thoroughly, when the footwear is dry. Oil-tanned leather can be kept in fine condition by such treatment, but will freeze stiff as a board in extreme cold. Smoke-tanned leather is the stuff for wear in very low temperatures.

Hobnails in boot soles are an abomination, except for lumberjacks and golfers. They hurt the feet when walking on hard surfaces, pick up all kinds of trash and are generally treacherous on rock. You can imagine what they do to tent floors and canoe bottoms. Mountaineers are supposed to favor them, traditionally, but many have been converted to composition soles in recent years. If I had to wear hobs or calks, I would use round-headed brass screws, with about three sharp calks in the instep of each boot for footing on logs.

Exercise the greatest of care in fitting boots for use on the trail. If too tight, they will cause you agony during a long march, and if too loose they will work up blisters. It is a pretty good scheme to try on new boots over two pairs of woolen socks, for a fairly snug fit. That will allow sufficient room for expansion as your feet spread out in the course of a hike, unless your arches flatten out completely. If you are troubled with weak arches, get arch supports with your new boots, as you would with everyday street shoes. Change socks during a long trek, for relief from "hot foot."

To serve as camp slippers, "glove" rubbers are worthy of some consideration. They weigh very little and afford the advantage of being waterproof. A man may slip on a pair of these over his socks and walk about in the early morning dew dry-shod.

Spare footwear should be carried in a stout drawstring shoe bag, so that moisture and dirt will not soil or damage other items in the pack. A piece of discarded oilcloth is often used for this purpose, but is far heavier than the inexpensive cotton bags offered by most outfitters. They weigh about 3 ounces.

PANTS from a discarded business suit are favored by some for wear in the woods, but in general their material and construction leave something to be desired. They present the constant threat of bursting seams and popping buttons, also. It is far smarter to buy garments made especially for the hard usage and hearty activity of outdoor life and avoid the risk of sudden disaster. Hard-woven fabrics are best for the purpose, as they gather fewer burrs than softer stuff and resist snags and tears to better effect. Whipcord or twill is very good and the fine worsted used by the Army is just about ideal. Many favor the modern lightweight fabrics, such as Gale cloth and Byrd cloth, and others, denim, in the form of cowpunchers' overalls or Levis. Heavy wool is fine for sitting in a blind or on a runway, but is apt to be very bunchy in the crotch and uncomfortable for walking. Also, it dries very slowly after wetting. It is preferable to wear several layers of underwear, rather than heavier pants, for warmth.

CUFFS on a woodsman's trousers serve no purpose but to gather trash and retain unwanted moisture.

BREECHES are very neat, but not especially practical for a woodsman. They usually bind over the knees, especially when you are sitting in a canoe. Also, when tucked into boot tops they can make your legs unbearably hot and sticky, for want of ventilation.

Regardless of weather, after a thorough wetting take off your clothes, wring them out and put them on again — that is, if a dry change is not available.

SUSPENDERS do the best job of holding up pants and breeches with heavily laden pockets and afford more freedom of action than a tight belt serving the same purpose.

SHIRTS are made to suit any purse or purpose. The fine woolens, in coat style, are very handsome and serviceable, but require a long-sleeved undershirt beneath them if bugs are to be encountered. They are very comfortable in cold weather, however, as the collar may be unbuttoned to cool off an overheated neck. The turtle-neck sweater, once so highly favored by collegians, offers no such advantage and is a most annoying chafer of day-old beards, to boot. The pull-over, with crew neck, long sleeves and knitted wristlets, is a favorite for moderate weather. In summer, I wear a pre-shrunk cotton sweat shirt of this model, the long, tight sleeves and the thick fabric offering fine defense against black flies and mosquitoes. It absorbs perspiration quite efficiently, washes easily and requires no ironing for neat appearance. A woolen version affords good comfort on chilly days.

A JACKET is required by most sportsmen, for protection against wind, rain and changes in temperature. Get one that will survive pretty rough usage, so you may toss it around in canoe or camp without fear of damage. It should have four pockets, with button-down flaps or zipper closures to prevent loss of odds and ends, and be long enough to cover the small of your back when sitting. Wool is the most satisfactory material, except in summer, when some light, tough fabric will be more comfortable. A buttoned front is generally more convenient than a zipper.

Jackets filled with eider down are offered in many styles and provide a maximum of cold-weather protection at minimum weight. It would be hard to imagine anything more comfortable for sitting in a frosty blind or on a windy runway, but for all-around service such a garment is too easily damaged. Good ones are quite expensive, too, which eliminates them from the ordinary camper's consideration.

Any jacket may become a nuisance when a hot ten-o'clock sun begins to dispel the early morning chill. If you are on foot and a long way from your base at such a time, you have to choose between the discomfort of wearing the coat and the inconvenience of carrying it. An improvised pack harness of heavy cord or light rope could serve to make the rolled-up garment a little back pack, out of the way and instantly ready for use in the cool evening. Two 4-foot pieces of clothesline would do the trick and add but little in bulk and weight to your equipment.

A HAT affords the best head covering in any but frosty weather, as its brim shades the eyes and neck from hot sunlight and serves to drape a head net away from the face. A light treatment of liquid waterproofing will benefit any hat worn for outdoor work.

BELTS with zipper-closed pockets for folding money are on the market and you'll find one of these very satisfactory for general use.

A KERCHIEF for your neck helps prevent bug bite and sunburn. It should be plenty large — say 24 inches square — and made of soft cotton or silk. The bandanna patterns, in red or blue, are most practical. Use the kerchief to tie down your hat on windy days.

GLOVES are pretty much of a necessity for the camper and will prevent many a blister and sliver in addition to defeating the fell purpose of black flies and mosquitoes. Stout buckskin, or other leather guaranteed to dry out soft after a wetting, is the proper material.

SPARE CLOTHING should be kept to a minimum on any camping trip. It is well enough to provide for every contingency, but an oversupply of miscellany soon gets to be a nuisance in camp, not only to the owner, but to his companions also. A few changes of underwear and socks, several handkerchiefs, an extra shirt, pair of pants, sweater and a change of footwear are about all that need be con-

Poncho

sidered. If your outing is to be of some duration, include a cake of naphtha soap and some clothespins and plan to do a bit of laundry work occasionally. A drawstring bag, pillow slip or clean flour sack will carry spare clothing very nicely.

THE PONCHO is your best bet for rain protection. It is nothing more or less than a waterproof sheet, with a slot in the middle for your head to go through. As a rain cape, it will drape over a pack on your back, cover your knees when you are sitting in a boat and allow plenty of ventilation. In camp, you can use it as a ground cloth, a cover for browse bags full of wet leaves, or a cooking shelter. Two ponchos, fastened together, make a shelter cloth that is well-nigh indispensable when camping with a crawl-in tent. The best size for a poncho is the largest offered — 66 × 90 inches. I like the Alligator material better than any other, as lighter-weight stuff will not stand as much abuse. You'll find it handy to work in three extra grommets on each long side and at least one on each short side of any poncho you buy, as the manufacturers have seen fit to furnish grommets only at the corners.

Light Equipment

You'll need some light equipment to be carried on your person constantly, and the following list will give you a good idea of what this should be:

KNIFE, in pocket or belt sheath. One good blade is all you require in the woods and it need be no longer than 3½ inches. A sheath knife, however, balances better with 4- or 4½-inch blade and you can carry that much steel without appearing armed for combat. Some states and provinces class blades longer than 4½ inches as weapons and you should bear that in mind when making your choice.

There is no reasonable purpose in carrying a small sword at your belt, unless a machete or brush knife is essential. Game and fish may be dressed most efficiently with a modest blade and if bread or bacon has to be sliced you can cut

Scout knife

down the middle of the chunk and then slice the halves with a pretty short piece of steel. No knife blade, however large, will replace the smallest ax when chopping is to be considered. The Boy Scout pocket knife is a very worthwhile implement, affording a large cutting blade, screw driver and bottle cap lifter, can opener, and leather punch in reasonable dimensions and weight. The Girl Scout model is similar, but smaller.

MATCHSAFE, of waterproof construction, even if you carry a cigarette lighter. Fill it with matches.

COMPASS. The floating dial model with luminous figures is best, I think.

BILLFOLD for game license, identification, and so on.

PURSE for small change.

POCKET WATCH of inexpensive make.

WHISTLE for signaling companions or calling dogs.
NOTEBOOK AND PENCIL.
MAP of the country to be traveled.

Compak snake-bite kit

SNAKE–BITE KIT of the COMPAK model, if in snake
country. The kit in camp will do you no good if you have to
walk to it.

FISHLINE AND HOOKS, on a bit of cardboard or wood,
in case you have to, or want to, fish unexpectedly. Thirty
feet of casting line, 6 or 8 feet of artificial gut leader,
6 assorted hooks and a few split shot should be enough. For
catching bait, a length of stout thread and a few tiny

minnow hooks with the barbs filed half off would be a valuable addition.

HANDKERCHIEF, red or blue, as a flash of white in the woods might encourage some fool to shoot you for a high-tailing deer, during hunting season.

PACK OF TOILET PAPER, in a neoprene tobacco pouch.

INSECT REPELLENT in a pocket-size container is a must in bug season. There are good pastes and better liquids, ready prepared, for sale in the better stores and you should have little trouble finding a preparation for use on your skin.

A TOILET KIT for camping is easily assembled and may be filled out or reduced as your requirements vary. The following items, dropped in a small bag or rolled up in the towel, will suffice for most excursions:

Comb
Toothbrush in a tube or box
Small tube of tooth paste
Razor
Razor blades
Shaving brush and soap (best for week-old beards)
Small metal mirror
Toilet soap in a box
Towel

A FIRST–AID KIT for personal use may be quite simple and compact. When weight is of no special importance, you might consider such items as:

Readi bandages
Tincture of iodine
Unguentine
New Skin
Soda bicarbonate
Tweezers

Cathartic pills
Corn pads
Aspirin
Spirits of camphor
Suppositories
Adhesive tape
Small scissors
Pomade, for chapped lips

Pack your selection in a cigar box or something similar. I sometimes use an old collar bag for the purpose.

Sharpening a knife or ax blade

BLADE ▨▨▨▨▨▨ WHETSTONE

Some sort of repair kit is needed in every camper's outfit, to care for damaged clothing and equipment. An assortment of some of the following may be carried in a small bag:

Buttons
Needles, large and small
Stout thread
Shoelaces
Rubber patches and cement
Wire-cutting pliers
Screw driver
Whetstone

Ferrule cement
Rod guides and tips
Can of oil
Gun grease
Jointed gun-cleaning rod
Twine
A few nails
2 or 3 screw hooks for clothes hangers
Small file

You may assume that hanging and storage space will be scant, in most any camp, so make your outfit as compact as possible.

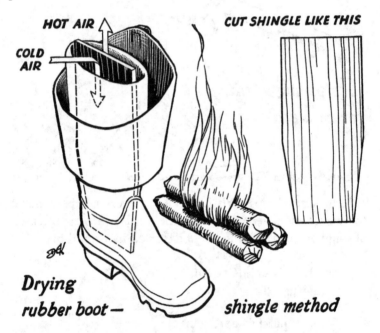

HOT AIR

COLD AIR

CUT SHINGLE LIKE THIS

Drying rubber boot —   *shingle method*

Keep your things in order at home and afield, so that everything will be easy to find and ready to pack.

Make such repairs as may become necessary at the first

opportunity, as a matter of preparation for some quick start in the future. Keep your cutlery sharpened.

Take every means to prevent moths, dry rot, mold or rust from destroying your precious equipment. Put everything away clean and dry, for storage between seasons.

Rubber boots, in particular, will stand close inspection for inside dampness. To dry them most easily, insert a shingle, or similar piece of lumber, in each leg; edges toward heel and toe. Do a little whittling, if necessary, to get a fairly tight fit from about knee high to the insole. With the shingles in place, stand each boot upright before a source of heat. The heat will cause the air to rise, on the near side of the shingle, sucking fresh air down on the other side and thus creating a current which will dry out boot feet better than any other system I know. Don't place the boots so close to fire as to scorch them.

Weapons and Tackle

If your first trip to camp happens to involve an initial attempt at hunting or fishing, choose your gun or tackle with the greatest care. You will do better to get equipment designed to serve faithfully for years to come, rather than invest in cheap merchandise which will neither please you nor develop your skill.

So far as guns are concerned, I think it an excellent idea to rent your first one, as it may prove unsuitable. Once you learn your own particular requirements, you can acquire a weapon to fit them.

Rifles

The sporting rifle is a precision instrument which should be selected for specialized work. For instance — you cannot expect to make clean kills on squirrels and deer with the same rifle, or bring down moose with a weapon designed for use on woodchucks. There are many tales of such feats, but mighty little tangible evidence. So make up your mind about what you intend to hunt and get a rifle to suit the purpose.

There are numerous models and calibers to choose from and an encyclopedia could be written on their various characteristics, but I'll treat only a few of the most popular.

The .22-caliber is your best bet for short-range target work and killing of small game such as squirrels. The "long rifle" cartridge affords best results with this arm. For plinking or other casual practice, .22 "shorts" and "longs" serve well enough, but they are not suitable for use on game. The same may be said of .22-shot cartridges, which are loaded primarily for shooting of small specimens by ornithologists, I believe.

For killing deer in wooded country, where long shots are rare, the .30–30 is just about standard equipment. The cartridge is most effective when loaded with a 170-grain bullet and I recommend the use of no other, regardless of published ballistics apparently favorable to lighter bullets.

A comparatively new cartridge, the .257 Roberts, is becoming increasingly popular for use on such quarry as woodchuck, coyote and fox. Some experts claim it to be highly effective on deer, but I prefer a heavier load for animals of such size and vitality. To me, it seems senseless and cruel to chance a less than fatal wound for the sake of theory.

The .270 Winchester has been proved very effective on large game, its high velocity and flat trajectory affording great shocking power and accuracy at extreme ranges. The .270 cartridge is loaded with either one of two standard bullets — 130-grain or 150-grain, the 130-grain load offering the best combination of characteristics, according to majority opinion. In the estimation of many who have used both weapons, the .270 outranks the famous .30–06, performance being equal in most respects and the lighter recoil of the .270 affording a definite advantage.

Personally, I find the .348 Winchester highly satisfactory for use on deer, bear and moose in heavily wooded country. Certainly it is no long-range weapon, as trajectories are quite high beyond 300 yards, and the lever action design is far from ideal for telescope mounting. The 200-grain .348 bullet will knock a deer off his feet, however, and the 250-grain slug can put down a moose or bear at 200 yards. The lever action is far handier for me than any bolt action I have yet found and the recoil is not nearly so vicious as that of the .30–06.

The .30–06 is, of course, one of the most deservedly popular calibers in use today. It has killing power, range and accuracy and may be had in many makes and models, and .30–06 ammunition is universally distributed, affording the great advantage of ready supply.

For successful killing of really big game, such as Alaskan brown bear or grizzlies, I think the practical hunter should seriously consider the .375 Magnum. Frankly, I have never used the weapon, but its shocking power is undoubtedly greater than that of any other standard American rifle, and shocking power in big doses is certainly a specific for extremely dangerous animals.

To sum up, briefly, before getting into further discussion, my recommendation is that you arm about as follows:

For squirrel, rabbit, etc.	.22 long rifle
For woodchuck, coyote, fox, coon, etc.	.257 Roberts
For deer and small bear at short range	.30–30
For deer, moose and bear at medium range	.348, .30–06 or .270
For elk, mountain sheep and deer at long range	.270 or .30–06
For grizzly, Alaskan and polar bear	.375 Magnum

There are many calibers, other than those mentioned, which perform very satisfactorily, and it is interesting to compare their ballistics in the elaborate tables issued by cartridge makers and gun dealers. You might acquire a few such publications for spare-time reading.

Factory sights on standard guns are worthy of a fair trial. You'll know more about special sighting requirements after rather extensive use of a new weapon.

The sighting-in of a hunting rifle is a chore to be completed before you go after game. You should know exactly what you can do with your weapon in various circumstances. More often than not, your chances of a successful kill will depend on a quick guess at the range and an instantaneous calculation of the proper sight: point-blank, high or low. For this reason, most hunters in forests fix iron sights to shoot point-blank at about 100 yards, figuring that an error in their estimation of range, 25 yards or so one way or the other, will direct the bullet only an inch or two over or under dead center. Take, as an example, the ballistics of the popular but none-too-accurate .30–30, shooting its best bullet, the 170-grain. Theoretically, this bullet rises 1 inch above the line of sight, to center or zero at 100 yards. Thus, if you had the sights set to zero at 100 yards and held fine on a deer at 50 yards, the bullet should strike 1 inch above the line of sight. At 150 yards the bullet would strike about 3 inches below the line of sight. In either case, the deflection would not be enough to score a miss, provided you held true on a vital spot.

You can learn a great deal about ammunition and ballistics from the *Western Ammunition Handbook,* which the Western Cartridge Company, East Alton, Illinois, will send you free of charge, on request. I urge you to get a copy.

Carry your rifle in a good case, whenever possible, clean

A FEW BALLISTICS

Cartridge	Bullet Weight (Grains)	Muzzle Velocity	100 Yards Velocity	100 Yards Energy	Trajectory, in Inches 100 Yards	200 Yards	300 Yards
.22 Long Rifle	40	1375	1080	104	2.9	...	...
.257	87	3220	2770	1485	0.5	2.5	6.0
.257	100	2900	2530	1420	0.6	2.5	7.0
.257	117	2630	2330	1410	0.7	3.0	8.0
.270	130	3120	2880	2395	0.5	2.0	5.0
.270	150	2770	2490	2065	0.6	3.0	7.0
.30—30	170	2200	1930	1405	1.0	4.5	12.0
.30—06	150	2960	2720	2465	0.5	2.5	6.0
.30—06	180	2690	2500	2500	0.6	3.0	7.0
.30—06	220	2410	2190	2345	0.8	3.5	9.0
.348	200	2520	2160	2075	0.8	4.0	10.0
.348	250	2320	2046	2380	0.9	4.2	10.8
.375	235	2860	2520	3315	0.6	2.5	7.0
.375	300	2540	2290	3495	0.7	3.5	8.5

Velocity is speed, in feet, per second.
Energy is striking force, in foot pounds.
Trajectory is height above line of sight at mid-range.

it often and lubricate it lightly with high-grade gun oil. Take your cleaning kit to camp with you and use it frequently.

Shotguns

Standard shotguns are offered in many different models and gauges, at prices to suit nearly any purse. It is impossible to select one gun entirely suitable for every sporting purpose, but you can acquire an arm adapted to a wide range of shooting requirements if you know what to look for. The average sportsman owns but one shotgun and uses it quite successfully on every kind of game from rabbits to geese, as occasion demands.

Unless you have a decided preference for smaller bores, a 12-gauge gun is the most practical choice, since 12-gauge ammunition may be found at any country store or backwoods trading post, but the less popular 16- and 20-gauge loads enjoy no such universal distribution. Obviously, this is of considerable advantage to a shooter who cannot conveniently carry all the ammunition he may need for an extended expedition.

For all-round shooting, the double gun affords several desirable features not found in single-barreled weapons. For instance, one barrel may be bored for open patterns and the other for concentrated patterns (modified choke and full choke, as an example). Or you may charge one barrel with loads designed to give wide patterns at close ranges (Thicket, Brush, Scatter, Spreader, and so on) and the other with longer-range ammunition.

"Choke" is the constriction of a shotgun barrel at or near the muzzle, designed to control the pattern or spread of the short charge. There are many variations of the choke, the most common being:

Full
Improved modified
Modified
Improved cylinder
Cylinder

These pattern about as follows:

Full choke   65–75 per cent of shot in 30-inch circle
                              at 40 yards
Improved modified   55–65 per cent of shot in 30-inch circle
                              at 40 yards
Modified   45–55 per cent of shot in 30-inch circle
                              at 40 yards
Improved cylinder   35–45 per cent of shot in 30-inch circle
                              at 40 yards
Cylinder   25–35 per cent of shot in 30-inch circle
                              at 40 yards

Stock guns in double-barreled models are ordinarily bored with one barrel full-choked and the other modified, but you can get just about any combination on special order. My advice is to get a stock model and pattern each barrel with a variety of loads, to discover the ammunition which will give the most desirable results. You may take it for granted that no two guns, similarly bored, will shoot exactly alike.

Barrel length is of no especial importance, so far as shooting results are concerned, the long barrel being favored by some because of its longer sighting plane and the short barrel by others for the sake of faster handling. Stock models generally run 26 inches and 30 inches in barrel length, but you can often find 28's and 32's, as well. To me, balance and fit appear more important than length of barrel.

Find a gun that feels right and sights naturally when you raise it to firing position, and you will not be far from a correct choice. A really good salesman or thoroughly experienced friend can readily check it for proper stock length and "drop," if there is any question about such features.

Ammunition is most important to a shotgun shooter and you should have some idea of the proper loads to be used in different circumstances. I have already mentioned Thicket loads and the like, which ordinarily are charged with 1⅛ ounces of number 6 or 7½ shot for upland game, such as quail and grouse. Pheasants, prairie chickens and ducks are more readily stopped with 1¼-ounce loads of number 5 or 6 shot, while geese and turkeys require number 2's or BB's with heavy charges of powder behind them. Make a practice of buying none but standard brands of ammunition and you'll soon discover the loads best suited to your gun and your sport.

Avoid guns with Damascus barrels. These were built for use with black powder and will not safely handle modern loads. You can lose a finger or an eye all too easily when a gun barrel bursts, and for that reason no chances should be taken with imperfect weapons. Plugged barrels are especially dangerous; so if you drop your gun in snow or mud make sure that barrels are clean before you fire them.

Any shotgun deserves cleaning and light lubrication after a day afield and clean, dry storage between seasons. A good carrying case for the gun will save it from many a scuff and scar.

Get this one thought firmly fixed in your mind before taking any weapon into the woods:

Your gun can kill or maim a human being!

Just one careless discharge may ruin your sport forever and put a blight on your entire life.

Be careful! Be Awfully Careful!

Learn to handle your gun with natural ease in every circumstance. Make a religion of safety. Be sure that you always know where your bullets may go, regardless of excitement or accident. Don't carry loaded weapons in a vehicle or into a building. Don't point a weapon, loaded or empty, at anything you don't want to kill or injure.

A safely carried gun

Fishing Tackle

Fishing tackle can run into heavy money, if you so desire, but a simple outfit will afford plenty of fun and excitement to begin with. I consider the following assortments ample for trail use:

Fly-Fishing Tackle

Fly rod, of split bamboo, 8 to 9 feet long, in three sections with extra tip. Weight, 4 to 5 ounces. Choose one with serrated ferrules and plenty of guides. Well-made rods usually have two guides on the butt joint, three on the middle joint and four or five on the tip. There should be guides quite close to the ferrules on every joint.

A tube of aluminum or other light, rigid material in which to carry the rod.

Tapered line, waterproofed, of the proper weight to be handled by your rod. Usually a 5-ounce rod with fairly stiff action will nicely handle an H D H line, but you will be wise to rely on the judgment of a good salesman or an experienced friend to pick out and match up a rod and line combination for you.

A fly rod reel, either single action or automatic, large enough to accommodate your line and of proper weight to balance your rod. It deserves a bag of its own to protect it from dirt.

Half a dozen tapered gut leaders, 9 feet long at least. Roughly, coarse leaders are used with large flies and in heavy water; fine leaders with small flies and in comparatively quiet water. Their purpose is to provide an invisible connection between your line and the fly. You could take three leaders tapered to 2x and three tapered to 4x and be fairly well equipped, but once again it would be far wiser to rely on the advice of an experienced friend.

An aluminum leader box, with thin felt pads to keep the leaders moist and pliable.

An assortment of flies — perhaps two or three dozen of various patterns and sizes, to start with. If you keep on fishing, you'll eventually gather hundreds of these and never be fully satisfied with the selection afforded. Depend, again, upon your experienced friend for advice on the initial assortment.

An aluminum fly box, with clips to hold several dozen flies separately.

A small, flat can of line dressing, similar to tallow, the purpose of which is to make the line float. Several standard brands are quite satisfactory.

A couple of dozen assorted split shot and a number of 8, 10 and 12 size trout hooks, in a plastic tube or tin box, may provide good worm fishing, if you are unsuccessful with flies.

All of the above, except the rod, will carry well in a small zipper bag, which, in turn, will offer fewer lumps and corners, in the pack, than a tackle box.

A landing net and a canvas creel complete the outfit.

FLY-FISHING TACKLE WEIGHTS

	Ounces
Automatic reel and tapered line	11
(Single-action reel with tapered line weighs only 5 ounces, if you prefer it.)	
Fly box (aluminum) filled	4¼
Leader box (aluminum) filled	1½
Spinner box (aluminum) filled	3
Line dressing	1¼
Split-shot hooks, etc., in tin box or plastic tube	1
Zipper bag	2
Fly rod in an aluminum tube	16
Folding landing net, suitable for small trout	9

If you expect to wade trout streams and cannot carry waders, take along a pair of rubber-soled canvas gym shoes, weighing about 2 pounds, and a pair of light cotton pants, weighing about a pound. You can wade recklessly in these and dry them easily.

You might well read Ray Bergman's fine book, *Trout,* before you get much beyond dreaming of fly-fishing.

Bait Casting Tackle

Jointed casting rod, of split bamboo, 4½ or 5 feet in length. Get a good one, with locking reel seat, agate tip and at least one agate guide nearest to the reel seat. Jointed steel rods are rarely flexible enough for good casting.

Multiplying reel, level-winding, capable of handling at least 50 yards of 18-pound test line.

A stiff leather case for the reel.

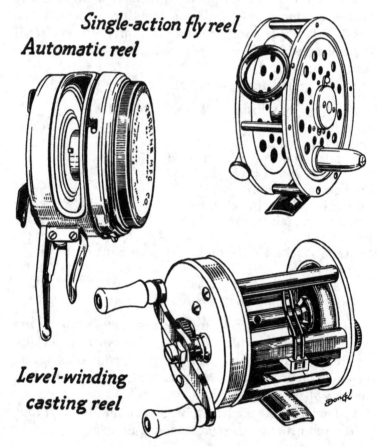

Single-action fly reel

Automatic reel

Level-winding casting reel

Fifty yards of braided silk casting line, about 10- or 12-pound test for bait casting, or 18-pound test if you intend to troll more than cast. It's a good idea to take two lines, in case you break one or decide to change your mode of fishing.

Four casting baits, in individual cardboard boxes or plastic tubes.

Six trolling spinners in a tin or cardboard box.

Twenty-four eyed hooks, of several sizes, including tiny minnow hooks, in a tin box or plastic tube.

Six gut leaders, in bass size.

Ten yards of artificial gut leader, 10- or 12-pound test.

Aluminum leader box, with felt pads to keep leaders moist and pliable.

An assortment of sinkers and 4 wire leaders in a plastic tube.

A bottle of pork rind bait.

All of this, except the rod, carries well enough in a small zipper bag, as does the fly tackle previously mentioned.

A landing net would be a good addition to the outfit and it would not be amiss to provide an aluminum tube or similar rigid case for protection of the rod.

BAIT-FISHING TACKLE WEIGHTS

	Ounces
Reel and 50-yard line, in leather case	14
6 spinners, in tin box	2
4 plugs, in cardboard box	3
50 yards of spare line, on spool	2½
24 eyed hooks, in tin box or plastic tube	1
Leader box (aluminum) filled	1½
Sinkers and wire leaders, in plastic tube	4
Pork rind, in bottle	6½
Zipper bag	3
5-foot jointed bait rod, in an aluminum tube	16

Of course, there are many kinds of fishing and very many kinds of tackle, which I shall not attempt to mention here. Discover for yourself what prospects are offered in the region to be visited and equip accordingly. My lists are intended mostly as reminders.

Bedding

Having acquired a serviceable outfit of personal equipment and some skill in its use, you are prepared for plain and fancy camping in established facilities. By adding a bedroll, you might very well qualify as a trail companion and cut in on an occasional expedition off the beaten path.

The importance of ample bedding cannot be overemphasized. Forest nights are often damp and cold, even in summer, and no campfire will make up for the lack of good warm covers. Nor will the carpet of pine needles which feels so soft and spongy to your feet afford a restful couch.

It is a common enough fallacy to assume that any healthy man can wrap himself in a single blanket and sleep like a babe on bare ground, if he is tired. It ain't so! Nor is it true that a camper's resting place may easily be cushioned with spruce boughs, or moss, or leaves. He needs plenty of cover and a good mattress if he intends to avoid the torture of restless nights.

If you have any illusions about this, sleep in your back yard a couple of nights. The experience may save some hard-won trip from complete ruin.

Take it for granted, then, that provision for peaceful sleep is essential to the success of any expedition. Consider that something like one third of your time will be spent abed and give the sleeping equipment a correspondingly important place in the outfit. You'll not regret the price exacted in weight and bulk.

For cover, blankets are pretty hard to beat. Afield, they will afford the advantage of adjustment to varying temperatures and at home stand some chance of meriting the housewife's loving care. You may be smart enough to justify the purchase of a sixty-dollar eider-down sleeping bag, even though your good spouse could use the money with greater satisfaction, but I would rather gamble on a pair of Hudson Bay Four Pointers, which, at least, can grace the guest room between trips.

Be that as it may, two blankets are warmer and handier than a single cover of equal weight. More often than not, you will be comfortable enough on retiring, but require more or less warmth along in the night. With a single heavy blanket, or a sleeping bag, you have no means of varying your covers, except by putting on or taking off clothing, which, of course, many practical woodsmen do.

Blankets should be plenty big enough to wrap around you and tuck in generously under the feet. My idea of the minimum size for comfort is 72 x 84 inches, unless you are fairly small and have no intention of ever sharing covers with a shipwrecked friend. Unless you can afford camel hair, 100 per cent virgin wool is the proper stuff for blankets.

I figure that a camel-hair blanket can be about one pound lighter than a woolen one and afford the same warmth, but have yet to reach the state of affluence necessary to actual experience.

Eider-down quilts are much warmer, per pound of weight, than either camel hair or wool, but require the greatest precaution against wet.

Many pretty pictures have been published to illustrate the joys and comforts of a sleeping bag with waterproof and bug-proof hood over the occupant's head. Theoretically, you can plunk down anywhere with one of these, and be as snug as the proverbial "bug in a rug" in no time at all.

These illustrations fail to depict the plight of the sleeper who literally "stews in his own juice" under the watertight cover on a hot night, or wakes in a pouring rain to wonder about getting his boots on. Any little tent and blanket combination beats such a rig and usually weighs less, in the bargain.

If you get a sleeping bag, choose one filled with eider down or wool. Ordinary feathers are quite heavy and none too warm and kapok is about on a par with cotton. Don't forget that the zipper which adds so much to the coziness of a bag can go utterly haywire and leave you definitely untucked-in. Snap fasteners will stand more hard wear.

Don't fool yourself with a pint-size sleeping bag. When you "hit the sack" after a hard day afield, you'll want stretching room in your bed. Leg muscles, in particular, will demand considerable flexing, which a snug bag will not accommodate. Nor will it allow you to roll and turn with freedom. Even in the yard-wide standard bag, a man has to press the bottom to the ground with his hands, before turning over, and if you have an air mattress stuffed into the pocket usually provided, the performance takes on complications.

When you shop for a sleeping bag you'll find some designed for moderate temperatures and others for extreme cold. Obviously, none of these will be entirely satisfactory for general use. If you intend to sleep out in all kinds of weather and can afford but one bag, I recommend medium weight. Blankets may be added when greater protection is required.

The business of stuffing a blanket into a sleeping bag can be most exasperating and futile, too, unless performed with some skill. The method illustrated may seem unduly complicated, but it is the only feasible one I have discovered. Fold the blanket lengthwise and turn over an 18-inch lap

at one end. (This will be at the foot of your bed.) Fold
again, lengthwise, and double over, end to end. This will
give you a pack about 18 by 36 inches, which may be laid
in the sleeping bag with the 18-inch lap at the foot and the
folds on the center line. Now, unfold the blanket so that
it lies doubled in the bag, neatly tucked in at the bottom.
You can have quite a time for yourself trying this with two
blankets, but it can be done if they are folded together.

Consider a small pillow for your sleeping outfit, if you

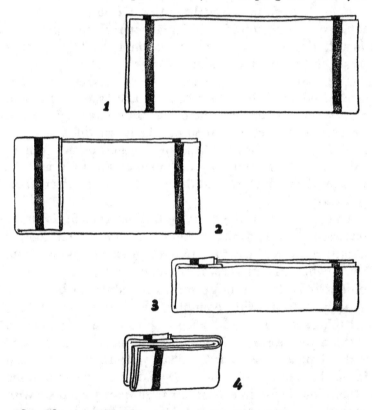

Stuffing a blanket into a sleeping bag

ordinarily use one. The clothing bag will be a mediocre substitute.

A knitted cap is fairly important to your sleeping comfort, although a large kerchief tied over your head will also serve to keep off ground drafts.

Changing into dry, clean underwear before going to bed is a wholesome and restful practice. Excess perspiration in your sleeping garments will cause "clamminess" and sometimes bring on chills.

If you happen to be caught out on a cold night with insufficient covers, consider taking a hot rock into bed with you. It might be wrapped in an empty duffel bag or a jacket to prevent too intimate contact.

The traditional woodsman's bed, of balsam branchlets stacked neatly under a tent floor, is a thing of beauty and a joy forever — until you lie on it for seven or eight hours. Properly constructed, it requires about ten times as much material as you might imagine and an hour or two of skillful labor. Often, you may find neither the time nor the balsam when you most need them, and so I recommend that you carry a bed.

Your best bet, in the portable bed department, is an air mattress. Used on a cot, or the top side of a forest floor, it affords more real comfort and rest than any other thing you might carry in a pack. Get one large enough to support your body. If you are small or medium in build, the 25 x 75 inch size will be ample. If you are a 200-pounder, get the 32 x 75 size. The knee-length models serve only to cushion your torso, and are not worth much consideration. Take along a small pump to inflate your mattress, although it may be blown up by lung power, at the expense of some exhaustion. Pump in enough air to support your body with buttocks barely off the ground. More will make the mattress roll and tend to slide out from under you, but adjustment may easily be accomplished with the filler valve, as you lie in bed and get the feel of the thing.

If you must forego the comforts of an air mattress, for one reason or another, the browse bag has possibilities as a substitute. In use, it is stuffed with balsam, fir or spruce branchlets, devoid of heavy stems, or less desirable padding such as dry grass, ferns or leaves.

A suitable bag is not too difficult to make. Four and one quarter yards of some light, tough fabric, about 40 inches in width, would be sufficient for a bag 36 × 75 inches, with boxed sides and one boxed end. Aberlite tent cloth would fill the bill nicely, and afford the pleasing advantage of a waterproof container for wet browse. In the dimensions given, an Aberlite bag would weigh about 2 pounds, complete with 6 large safety pins to close the open end. You could save a few ounces by cutting the width of the bag to 30 inches or so.

Cambric, such as handkerchiefs are made of, works up into a satisfactory lightweight bag, if treated with Rainy Day, Protectol, or other good waterproofing.

When bulk is of no especial importance, a good, thick wool quilt might be substituted for some other form of mattress. Its chief disadvantage would spring from the problem of keeping it dry, as once thoroughly wetted a quilt is useless for days on end.

I have a pad, filled with kapok and tufted crosswise to prevent shifting and wadding of the filler. It leaves a lot to be desired as a camp mattress, but something similar, stuffed with about four pounds of wool batt and waterproofed, should make a pretty fair bed. It would afford the advantage of being always ready for use and might possibly eliminate the weight of one blanket. The next time I have the misfortune of losing an air mattress, I'm going to experiment with the pad.

III

CAMPING EQUIPMENT

Sooner or later, the fellow who has enjoyed a few trips to established camps will get to dreaming of expeditions farther afield. Wilder scenery, bigger game or more plentiful fish may be the lure, or perhaps he will desire nothing more than greater scope of activity. Anyhow, his thoughts will turn to an outfit: tent, cooking kit and other accessories, sufficient to set up housekeeping where he will.

This is a most intriguing subject, which can afford the practitioner year-round fun and entertainment. Long winter evenings may be occupied most enjoyably working over the outfit — assembling kits of this and that or fashioning gadgets for next season's use. Outfitter's catalogues can be the most fascinating reading and stimulate the imagination when everything else fails utterly.

The prospective camper who enjoys the use of an automobile and a fairly robust bank balance can just about let himself run wild on equipment, if he so desires. Commodious tents, comfortable beds and elaborate cooking accessories are offered in a wide range of models, and such outright luxuries as iceboxes, portable showers and folding furniture are readily available.

This type of impedimenta works up into an outfit weighing hundreds of pounds, which may be used successfully only where ample transportation is available.

At the other extreme is the back-packer's snug little outfit, composed of tiny crawl-in tent, eider-down sleeping bag, pocket-size cook kit and very meager accessories.

In between are outfits suitable for hunters, canoe trippers and others who shift camp frequently and must tote their stuff into new territory.

I shall offer a few lists of equipment, comprising complete outfits for varied purposes. These are designed to cope with actual conditions to be expected in average camping territory, where fuel, browse and drinking water will be hard to find, more often than not. It is easy enough to figure out theoretical outfits of featherweight proportions, but don't fool yourself with such scheming. Poorly cooked meals, nights without adequate bedding and lack of proper shelter can and will deprive you of all the satisfaction of "going light" and most of your fun. On the other hand, it is all too easy to clutter an outfit with stuff that "might come in handy," but which will more surely break your back instead. I can't claim to be letter-perfect as an outfitter, but you'll find that the kits suggested will come pretty close to making you comfortable in ordinary circumstances.

Before we assemble an outfit, however, let us look over a few items of equipment recommended for general use.

Shelter

Shelter is an item which enthusiastic novices often slight. My first partner and I discovered, in just one awfully long night, that a simple square of canvas will not serve the purpose of a tent in summertime. Rain came in on us, mosquitoes gathered by the hundreds and crawling things wandered freely over and under our blankets. We made the canvas into a tent for our next venture into the woods, and screened it with cheesecloth, but rains soaked through the untreated fabric and bugs were soon flying, unhindered, through many

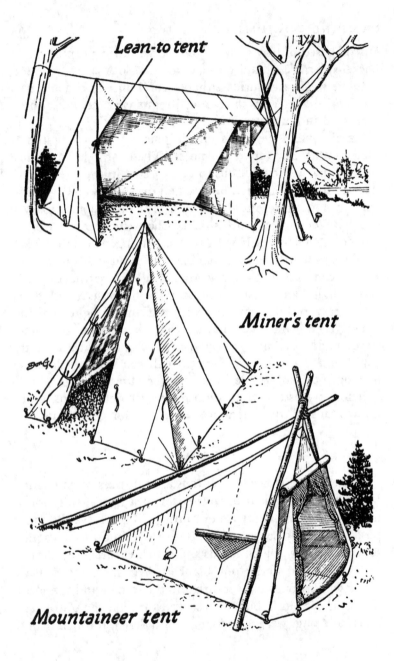

Lean-to tent

Miner's tent

Mountaineer tent

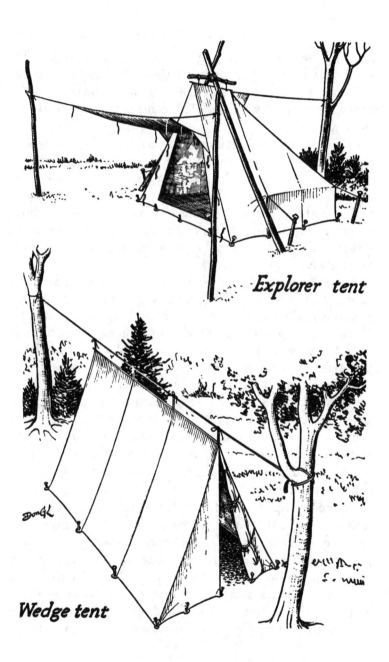

Explorer tent

Wedge tent

rents in our flimsy netting. The lack of a sewed-in floor invited ants and spiders to make themselves right at home and we were never without them, from the first day on. I think my partiality for late fall camping was engendered there and then.

By all means, give serious consideration to a tent which will afford protection from elements and pests. It should be really waterproof, stable and easy to manage. When bugs and snakes are to be expected, the tent should be equipped with sewed-in floor and excellent screening made of bobbinet or marquisette. In cold weather, no screening is required and a sewed-in floor becomes somewhat of a nuisance, as it collects pools of snow water.

There is no such thing as an all-purpose tent. If you can afford but one, decide, in a general way, on an outdoor program best suited to your conditions and equip accordingly. If winter appeals to you more than summer as a camping season, you must reckon with heating problems rather than bug defense, and vice versa.

Tents are manufactured in many models, ranging from tiny crawl-ins weighing less than 4 pounds to commodious wall tents suitable for permanent camps. Whatever model you choose, get it from a first-class dealer, whose experience and reputation will assure you of proper design, excellent materials and honest workmanship. A shoddy tent is no bargain at any price.

If your transportation facilities are not too limited, give serious thought to standing room and space to sit around in on rainy days. When the prospect of portaging and backpacking does not discourage it, I like to take a tent about 8 × 8 feet on the ground and 7½ feet high. In this, two men can sleep comfortably far apart, find room to dress and hang up clothing, keep their duffel inside, away from porcupines and rabbits, and loaf when the weather drives them under cover. For mild weather camping, a good number in this size is the Explorer model of Aberlite material, which weighs about 15½ pounds. It goes up fairly easily, with either shears or an inside pole, keeps out weather and pests and stays put in everything short of a gale. Its door canopy serves nicely as a cooking shelter.

The Cruiser tent is a smaller edition of the Explorer model, being 5 feet wide, 7 feet long and 5 feet high. It affords fairly ample shelter for two men and is a good bet for canoe travelers, as it weighs but 7½ pounds.

A very popular shelter is the A or wedge tent widely used by North Woods guides. It sets up best with shears and outside ridge, however, and the five poles required for such erection cannot always be found. The same is true of the wall tent and the Campfire or Baker model.

A Miner's tent, which is pyramidal in shape, sets up about the easiest of any, with one center pole and relatively few stakes. It affords good heat reflection from the campfire in cold weather, and will withstand a lusty wind, but is difficult to screen properly for summer use. Also, its doorway, opening nearly to the peak for reasons of ventilation, exposes considerable of the floor space to rain.

The Umbrella tent, greatly favored by auto campers, is very roomy, but also very heavy and tricky in high wind. It is impractical for canoeists and back-packers.

A lean-to tent will afford ample shelter and good heat reflection for fall camping and is very easy to transport, as it weighs but a few pounds. One of the best makers offers a model 6 feet wide, 6 feet 4 inches deep and 5 feet high, of Aberlite material, weighing 5 pounds. A ground cloth 6 × 7 feet will add 2½ pounds of weight, but serve also as a pack cloth or cooking shelter.

A pup tent will serve the simple purpose of protecting your bedding from rain if you are willing to forgo the com-

Campfire tent

Umbrella tent

fort and convenience of a larger shelter. Some models are equipped with screening and ground cloths.

The Mountaineer tent is a nifty little shelter, far better than any pup tent, but still too small for anything but mere protection.

All of these miniature tents have a tendency to wrap around you like a wet nightshirt, if you pack them tightly with a man rolled up in bedding.

To give you a clear idea of comparative weights, I detail the several models just mentioned:

Model	Material	Size in Feet			Weight in Pounds	Number of Stakes Required
		Width	Depth	Height		
Explorer	Egyptian	7⅓ ×	7⅓ ×	7½	15	19
Explorer	Egyptian	9¾ ×	7⅓ ×	7½	17½	21
Explorer	Extra Light	6½ ×	6½ ×	7	9	20
Explorer	Extra Light	8 ×	8 ×	7½	13	22
Explorer	Copperyacht	7½ ×	7½ ×	7½	17	19
Explorer	Copperyacht	9 ×	7½ ×	7½	24	21
Explorer	Aberlite	6½ ×	6½ ×	7	12	13
Explorer	Aberlite	8 ×	8 ×	7½	15½	17
Cruiser	Egyptian	5 ×	7 ×	5	7½	14
Cruiser	Extra Light	5 ×	7 ×	5	7	14
Cruiser	Copperyacht	5 ×	7 ×	5	9½	14
Cruiser	Aberlite	5 ×	7 ×	5	7½	14
* Miner's	Egyptian	7⅓ ×	7⅓ ×	7	7¼	12
* Miner's	Egyptian	9¾ ×	9¾ ×	8½	9¾	16
* Miner's	Extra Light	8 ×	8 ×	7½	6¾	20
* Miner's	Extra Light	9½ ×	9½ ×	8½	8¾	24
* Miner's	Copperyacht	7½ ×	7½ ×	7	10¾	12
* Miner's	Copperyacht	10 ×	10 ×	8½	14¾	16
* Miner's	Aberlite	6½ ×	6½ ×	7	6½	8
* Miner's	Aberlite	8 ×	8 ×	7½	8¾	12
* Wedge	Egyptian	7⅓ ×	7⅓ ×	7	9½	12
* Wedge	Egyptian	7⅓ ×	9¾ ×	7	11¼	14
* Wedge	Egyptian	9¾ ×	9¾ ×	8	14	16
* Wedge	Extra Light	6½ ×	6½ ×	7	6½	18
* Wedge	Extra Light	6½ ×	8 ×	7	8	20
* Wedge	Extra Light	8 ×	8 ×	8	9½	22
* Wedge	Copperyacht	7½ ×	7½ ×	7	13	12
* Wedge	Copperyacht	7½ ×	10 ×	7	15½	14

Model	Material	Size in Feet Width	Depth	Height	Weight in Pounds	Number of Stakes Required
* Wedge	Copperyacht	9 ×	11 ×	7½	18	16
* Wedge	Aberlite	6½ ×	6½ ×	7	8¼	10
* Wedge	Aberlite	6½ ×	8 ×	7	10	12
* Wedge	Aberlite	8 ×	8 ×	8	12¼	14
* Wedge	Aberlite	8 ×	9¾ ×	8	14	16
* Campfire	Egyptian	7 ×	7 ×	7½	11½	16
* Campfire	Egyptian	9¾ ×	7 ×	7½	13½	18
* Campfire	Extra Light	6½ ×	6½ ×	7	9½	20
* Campfire	Extra Light	8 ×	6½ ×	7½	10½	24
* Campfire	Copperyacht	7½ ×	7½ ×	7½	18¾	16
* Campfire	Copperyacht	10 ×	7½ ×	7½	21½	18
* Campfire	Aberlite	6½ ×	6½ ×	7	10¾	20
* Campfire	Aberlite	8 ×	6½ ×	7½	12	24
* Wall	Extra Light	6½ ×	6½ ×	6	7	28
* Wall	Extra Light	6½ ×	8 ×	6	8½	32
* Wall	Extra Light	8 ×	8 ×	7	10	36
* Wall	Extra Light	8 ×	9½ ×	7	11¼	40
* Wall	Extra Light	9½ ×	9½ ×	7½	13½	46
* Wall	Copperyacht	7½ ×	7½ ×	6½	16	20
* Wall	Copperyacht	7½ ×	10 ×	7	20	16
* Wall	Copperyacht	9 ×	11 ×	7½	29	24
* Wall	Copperyacht	10 ×	12⅓ ×	8	32	24
* Wall	Copperyacht	12⅓ ×	13½ ×	9	36	26
* Wall	Aberlite	6½ ×	6½ ×	6	8	14
* Wall	Aberlite	6½ ×	8 ×	6	9½	18
* Wall	Aberlite	8 ×	8 ×	7	11	20
* Lean-to	Aberlite	6 ×	6⅓ ×	5	5	8
† Umbrella	Coplin	8 ×	8		70	
† Umbrella	Coplin	10 ×	10		78	
Pup	Aberlite	5 ×	7 ×	3½	3½	
Mountaineer	Atomwate	4 ×	6½ ×	4	3¾	

* Weights of Miner's, Wedge, Campfire, lean-to, wall and pup tents do not include floors or mosquito netting.

† Weight of umbrella tent includes poles, stakes and one side curtain.

The Jungle Hammock is a combination of bed and shelter, developed during the war for use in tropical climates. It affords the possibility of a quick and easy setup, but has limitations which do not recommend it to all campers. For one thing, it must be slung from two stout trees, which may not always be found in the most desirable location. Also, there is little room in the hammock for duffel. It does provide a reasonably comfortable bed and shelter from weather and bugs, however.

Tent Materials

Mention has been made of several fabrics long since proved satisfactory for waterproof tents. In general, they are cotton cloths, treated with chemical compounds to make them water-repellent. Canvas has been given little consideration, because we have dealt with lightweight equipment and it is heavy stuff. It serves best in big tents, where large surfaces are exposed to wind and lighter material might take a fatal beating.

The time is coming, and shortly too, when rubberlike materials, such as neoprene, will offer advantages not to be overlooked by the camper. Considerable experimentation has already been made and there are tents of synthetic fabric now on the market. I find one fault with them: when tightly closed, they condense a lot of moisture, to plague the occupants. On the other hand, they appear to be impervious to mildew and will certainly shed rain.

There is a limit to lightness in tent material. The smallest shelter will catch plenty of wind, at times, which may rend flimsy fabric or tear out grommets and eyelets.

Incidentally, you may find it necessary to loosen guy ropes and stake ropes during heavy rain. Some are made of fibers which shrink when wet, to put heavy strain on material and fastenings. Untreated fabric may also shrink, to the same end.

The pack itself often damages light tents. Coarse fabrics used in duffel bags and the like will chafe more fragile stuff and sometimes wear holes in it. Guard against this possibility in packing and transport.

A TELESCOPING TENT POLE, of steel, is a major convenience when carrying facilities permit its use. The Explorer tent sets up with one, supplemented by a short, tubular ridgepole; the combination weighing 4 pounds 2 ounces. The pole for a tent 7½ feet high telescopes to 34 inches, just about right for carrying in an ordinary duffel bag. The ferrule which fits into the ridge can poke holes in all manner of things, but I find that a rubber fuller ball, such as is used for water faucet repair, will protect it quite neatly. Mine is tied to the pole with a few inches of fish line and, so far, has always been on hand to fit over the ferrule when needed.

Similar poles may be bought in pairs, with ridgepoles to match, for use with wall or wedge tents, but their weight is excessive. An 8 × 8 × 7 foot tent, for example, requires two uprights and a ridgepole, weighing, altogether, 12½ pounds.

Jointed poles, of lightweight alloy, are offered for use with small tents, 5 feet or less in height. A 5-foot pole of this kind, with ridge, sets up the Cruiser tent and weighs but 1½ pounds. The joints are 22 inches long, offering no packing problem.

TENT STAKES of steel or aluminum may be required if you expect to use popular camp sites in well-traveled territory. Former occupants may have burned all available sticks or branches. I find that nine 12-inch stakes and eight 9-inch stakes set my 8 × 8-foot Explorer tent quite satisfactorily on just about any forest floor. Made of aluminum, the 12-inch stakes weigh 2 ounces each and the 9-inch stakes 1¼ ounces each. I carry them in a canvas shoe bag and the entire package weighs but 2 pounds.

Ordinary stakes of wood, aluminum or iron are not rugged enough for use in frozen or stony soil. Timber spikes are best for such service. The 12-inch ones weigh about 6 ounces apiece and the 8-inch about 4 ounces.

In loose sand or very dry loam, no stake will hold effectively and you may find it necessary to tie the tent stake loops to logs or bundles of brush buried in the ground.

Cooking Gear

A CAMP COOK KIT differs from its kitchen cousin in that it must nest together, in compact form, for convenience in carrying. For that reason, handles, spouts and other sharp projections must be eliminated. For the sake of lightness, aluminum is favored as a material for camp utensils.

Assembled cook kit

A considerable variety of ready-assembled cook kits is offered by reputable vendors, together with supplementary pieces of similar design which may be assembled to suit your own fancy. Make your purchase with consideration for substantial material, absence of protruding bail "ears," portability and general usefulness. An excellent kit for two men consists of:

1 frying pan, with hinged handle, 8½ inches in diameter
1 stewpot, of 3¼-quart capacity
1 cover for the pot
1 coffeepot, of 2-quart capacity, with folding handles, very
  blunt spout and hinged cover
1 mixing pan, of 1¾-quart capacity, with folding handles
2 plates

All of this weighs but 3 pounds 6 ounces and nests into a
package 9 inches in diameter and 5½ inches high. It must
be supplemented, of course, with:

2 cups, preferably of enamelware, which will not burn the
  lips or cool the contents so readily as aluminum
2 spoons, cereal size, for greatest usefulness
2 table forks
2 table knives
1 salt shaker
1 pepper shaker
1 paring knife
1 pancake flapper, or spatula
1 can opener
1 canvas roll for the "tools"
1 empty friction-top can, for bacon grease
1 dish towel
1 dish rag, or mop
1 cake of naphtha soap, in a box or bag
1 dozen soap pads, for pot cleaning.

These items will add about 3 pounds to the kit, bringing
its total weight to 6 pounds 6 ounces and increasing its size
to about 9 × 9 inches.

You can cook and eat just about anything with an outfit
such as detailed, but considerable convenience may be
gained by adding:

	Ounces
1 frying pan	12
1 plate, for serving	3
1 measuring cup and spoon	3
1 mixing spoon	· 3
1 breadboard, 18″ × 12″, of plywood	16
1 slicing knife, in sheath	6
1 dish towel	3
2 hook-and-chain pot hangers	2
Total weight of additions	3 pounds

On the other hand, you may strip down the original kit, for light traveling, by eliminating:

	Ounces
Stewpot cover	3
Table knives	4
Salt and pepper shakers	1
Paring knife	4
Tool roll	3
Soap box	1
Thus saving just	1 pound

This stripped kit, as described, forces you to use sheath knives as cutlery, which is all right if you and your partner customarily wear them and are not finicky about eating with blades occasionally used for other purposes.

In my opinion, two small frying pans are better than one large one, as it is often convenient to cook certain foods, such as bacon and pancakes, in separate vessels.

The TOOL ROLL mentioned in my lists is more of a necessity than you might imagine. Make one of light canvas, with individual pockets for knives, forks, spoons and such. When each pocket is filled, you'll know nothing has been left behind. There should be a flap to fold over the pockets, and the hem of this should be left open, so that a stick may be run through it. Thus when you open out the roll, insert the stick and hang the kit on a tree, a miniature kitchen cabinet is in operation, for the cook's convenience. It will keep many a fork or spoon from being lost in the under-growth.

A REFLECTOR OVEN, or folding baker, provides the surest means of baking bread or biscuits on the trail. It bakes by reflecting heat from a near-by fire onto the top and bottom of a baking pan supported within its angle. The fire should be backed with a wall of small logs, stone or

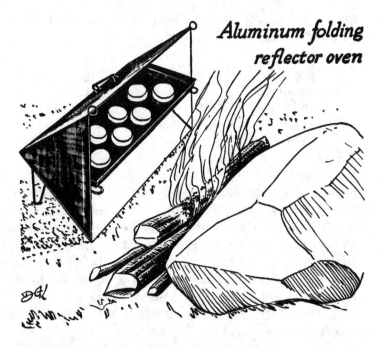

Aluminum folding reflector oven

earth, and a bit of experimentation is necessary to determine the proper distance of the baker from the fire. Standard models open to a width of 18 inches, height of 15 inches and depth of 8 inches, folding to 18 × 11 × 1 and weighing about 3 pounds.

A STOVE. is essential, in territories where decent fuel may be hard to find. The camper following a popular trail usually discovers that his predecessors have long since used all the desirable wood, leaving him nothing more than saplings and debris. Such stuff generally blazes too hotly, smokes

Primus stove

excessively and burns out completely, leaving no lasting bed of coals for steady cooking. In other regions, there simply is no good firewood and it is common practice for professional woodsmen to carry fire with them, when journeying there. The Primus, or Swedish pressure stove, has long been popular with trappers, surveyors and prospectors working the Far North, as it delivers a great deal of heat for its weight. In fact, one must regulate its blowtorchlike flame carefully, or run the risk of ruining aluminum utensils. The Primus stove is a one-burner affair, usually weighing about 2 pounds, and burns kerosene. The vaporizer should be preheated by burning more volatile fuel, preferably alcohol, in a cup built in for that purpose. The better-made Primus models will burn 2 hours on a pint of kerosene and boil a quart of water in less than 10 minutes.

A good practice is to carry this stove empty and the supply of fuel in screw-top cans or nonleaking canteens. A little engineering will enable you to fit stove, alcohol can and fuel containers into a tight tin, such as originally contained popcorn or pretzels. This will tend to prevent the kerosene from contaminating your food supply. The tin will serve handily as a dishpan or, on occasion, as an oven. Don't fail to take along a couple of the jet cleaners supplied with the stove.

My experience indicates that a man can cook coffee, bacon and cakes, for breakfast; boil tea for lunch; and prepare tea, stewed fruit, meat and potatoes for supper, with about 90 minutes of Primus use per day. This for two persons, by the way. Add 30 minutes for dishwater and happenstances and figure to use about a pint of fuel per day. A gallon of kerosene weighs $6\frac{7}{10}$ pounds and should be ample for a full week's cooking. Eight fluid ounces of alcohol, in a tin, should be enough primer for a week and will weigh about 10 ounces.

THE COLEMAN POCKET STOVE might be roughly termed a gasoline-burning version of the Primus. It, too, is a one-burner device, weighing 2 pounds when empty. The tank holds one pint of fuel, which will burn for more than 2 hours, under 20 pounds of air pressure, and bring a pint of water to boil in the first 7 minutes. The Pocket stove affords several advantages not to be found in the Primus. For one thing, it burns gasoline, which is a trifle lighter than kerosene and far less messy. It is more compact, also, and is sold complete with a two-piece container, which may serve nicely as pot and pan. The entire outfit, stove and container, weighs but 2 pounds 12 ounces and is $8\frac{1}{2}$ inches high by $4\frac{1}{2}$ inches in diameter. No can of primer is required by the Coleman stove, and some weight is thus saved.

The use of a one-burner stove requires some scheduling to make things come out right. For instance: breakfast should be prepared by making the coffee first, cooking the bacon next and the cakes or eggs last of all.

Pocket stove

Larger stoves may be carried, to good advantage, when weight is less of a factor. There are two-burner and three-burner gasoline stoves in many models, some of them equipped with folding ovens. Two-burner stoves weigh as little as 10 pounds and as much as 20. I have never yet found two gasoline stoves of different pattern burning fuel at the same rate. If you get one, experiment with it until you can figure how much fuel will be required for any proposed trip.

Any liquid-fuel stove will sometimes require a windshield,

when used out of doors. You may rig one with poncho, coat or pack cloth, when circumstances require such shelter, or take the cooking department right into the tent.

A very compact and practical source of cooking heat is afforded by the Speaker Heatab-Cookit. This consists of a white metal box, 4 × 3 × ¾ inches, containing a carton of chemical tablets; all of which weighs 5 ounces. The box opens up in such manner as to provide a stand for pot or pan and a base for the burning tablets. The supply of tablets is sufficient for 2 hours of minimum heat, or less if two or more are burned simultaneously for quicker cooking. One small tablet will burn 7 minutes and bring a half pint of water to a boil in that time. Three are required for similar results with a pint of water. Obviously, the preparation of a full meal would be very slow business with this device, but it surely is a natural for heating a can of soup or brewing a cup of tea in circumstances which afford no better facilities. Incidentally, Heatab tablets are dandy fire starters and a small carton of 15 weighs but 2 ounces.

Canned heat, or Sterno, also provides quick and easy fire for light cooking. It is marketed in friction-top tins of various sizes and the manufacturer offers several types of lightweight folding stoves for convenient use. A small can of Sterno contains 9½ ounces of the jellylike fuel and will burn for 90 minutes. Gross weight of can and contents is 12½ ounces. The Sterno flame requires 13 minutes to bring a quart of water to a boil and, as in the case of Heatabs, affords the prospect of pretty slow work on any extensive cooking. However, it is worthy of consideration for emergency jobs of heating.

Wood-burning stoves designed to be readily portable are offered by some outfitters. They provide for better cooking facilities than any open fire and are especially worthy of consideration for heating purposes. If you get one for use in a tent, be sure to provide a fireproof opening for the stovepipe. There are asbestos and metal rings made for the purpose and most tent makers will sew in one, on order. The stove should be long enough to accommodate fairly large billets of wood and be equipped with some means of draft regulation. A majority of wood-burning camp stoves are of the folding type, made of sheet steel. You may assume that any of them will warp, after use, often to the extent of making them pretty awkward to reassemble.

A pair of FIRE IRONS, made of ⅜ inch square steel, about 24 inches long, will serve nicely as a campfire grate and be much handier than a grate to carry. Laid across logs, stones or mounds of earth, they will support a frying pan and a coffeepot. With a canvas case they should weigh about 2 pounds per pair. A grate of similar weight would accommodate no more utensils and probably be so flimsy as to warp out of shape in no time at all.

CHAIN POT HANGERS take the place of dingle sticks,

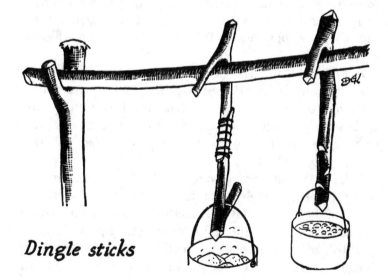

Dingle sticks

when dingle stick material cannot be found. You can make them of flat chain such as is used on bathtub plugs, attaching a hook of iron wire at each end. In use, you loop one end over your fire crane and the other through the bail of your pot, moving the hooks to different links of the chain for adjustment.

A piece of HEAVY SACKING, or burlap, about 4 feet square, will provide refrigeration for perishables, such as butter, meat and fish. Soak it in water, wring it out, wrap it around your food container and hang in a current of air. Evaporation of the water will absorb surplus heat from your food and help greatly to preserve it. When wet, the best place to carry it is on the outside of a pack or duffel bag. The cloth weighs about 1 pound, dry.

A TARPAULIN, large enough to shelter your cooking space, is a major convenience in any camp. Two ponchos, fastened together by a ridge rope run through the grommets, afford a good substitute, but necessarily deprive you of personal rain equipment when so used. If you can afford to carry extra weight, an 8 × 10-foot sheet of Aberlite, weighing about 4 pounds, is far handier. Have it liberally grommeted.

A TARP TENT, designed to set up as a pyramidal shelter 7 × 7 feet on the ground and 6½ feet high, serves both as extra tent for side trips and as tarpaulin. It is nothing more or less than a rectangle of cloth, 10 × 13 feet, with tent-stake loops attached in the proper places. Made of Aberlite, it weighs 6½ pounds.

MATCHES should be waterproofed for woods use. You may dip them in melted paraffin or thinned-out shellac, to accomplish this purpose. One method is to stick the matches in a soft cake of soap (heads up, of course), dip 'em in a shallow dish of the liquid waterproofing and set aside to dry. Choose matches with good sticks, to keep down the percentage of breakage. Carry them in a friction-top can or other container likely to remain watertight.

The use of FIRE STARTERS may seem a sissy business, until you have experienced a few desperate searches for tinder in wet woods. No doubt an expert woodsman should be able to make a fire in any circumstances, but there will be many occasions when time and temper may be saved to good advantage.

There are any number of fire starters on the market, one good one being a sawdust compound which looks like rough wall board. It is sold in a 12-ounce package containing 36 small pieces, each piece being sufficient to kindle one fire. The package measures $1\frac{5}{8} \times 2\frac{3}{4} \times 9\frac{1}{2}$ inches.

OLD TOOTHBRUSH HANDLES, of celluloid, make dandy fire starters and a dozen or so take up little room in a pack.

Two or three dried-out cedar shingles, or a whittling block of pine, have been found in many an old-timer's pack, for no other purpose than the provision of quick and easy tinder.

Tools

AN AX is considered a camp essential, although many hikers do without one, especially in summer. Available models are numerous, with champions for every one. In moderate weather I find a hatchet, or belt ax, with $1\frac{1}{4}$-pound head and 14-inch handle, most convenient, not only for wood chopping, but for rough carpentry as well. A heavier ax, say one with 3-pound head and 28-inch handle, is required if heating fires are to be maintained throughout long, cold nights — unless a saw is carried. Whatever model ax you choose, get the best quality and a leather sheath to cover the blade. Beware of your ax, it can be as dangerous as a cobra, in careless hands!

A CAMP SAW, on the order of a miniature cross-cut, with coarse teeth, is something to warrant earnest consideration. With such a tool, you can cut more wood, with less effort, than any expert ax man. Also, its use eliminates the danger of bad cuts and bruises from flying chunks. An over-all length of 27 inches is about right. A sheath to protect the blade is just about essential. The saw I use weighs 2 pounds 4 ounces, complete with leather sheath.

A TRENCHING SHOVEL, of army style, is well worth carrying on nearly any trip. On rainy nights, a trench must be dug on each side of the tent to prevent drainage into your abode, and nothing quite replaces a shovel for such work. Again, you may require a bean hole, a can of worms, a latrine or a garbage dump, all of which are difficult to excavate with makeshift tools. The shovel is also a fine fire tool, when used to transfer coals from your main blaze to the cooking setup. You'll need a sheath for the blade, to prevent cutting of pack sacks. Shovel and webbing sheath weigh 1 pound 15 ounces.

Lights

LAMPS and LANTERNS are of many styles and patterns, the most convenient being those operated by electricity. One popular model in this category may be used as a searchlight or a standing lamp and weighs but 1 pound, ready for action. With reasonable use, its batteries will last through a two-weeks trip. A pair of spare batteries weighs 7 ounces and may be carried indefinitely, without much deterioration, if kept dry.

CANDLES are favored by many campers, as they never deteriorate unless broken or eaten by mice. They serve best in a folding candle lantern or an empty can rigged as a reflector and wind guard. So far as I have been able to discover, flashlight batteries and candles give about the same number of hours of light, pound for pound.

KEROSENE is a good old source of light, but it is a nuisance to carry, as one drop will contaminate any amount of food. Lantern chimneys are easily broken, too.

ACETYLENE LAMPS give lots of light and are handy to carry, but require recharging for each period of use. Once the carbide is activated with water, it keeps on giving off gas until exhausted, whether you use the gas or not.

MANTLE LANTERNS, burning gasoline vapor, are very fine for fixed camps, but difficult to transport safely. The fuel is apt to spoil some of your grub, also, as in the case of kerosene.

I like to carry a small flashlight for puttering around after dark and a couple of candles for tent illumination, although both are sometimes left out of my kit when weight must be kept to a minimum.

Packing Accessories

ALUMINUM CANS, with screw tops, are fine for carrying butter and lard. The ordinary size, $3\frac{1}{2} \times 4\frac{1}{2}$ inches, holds a pint of liquid or a pound of butter, and weighs $2\frac{3}{4}$ ounces. Be sure to sterilize such a container, with boiling water, before putting butter in it. If you use powdered milk, an extra butter can serves mighty well as a mixing vessel.

FOOD BAGS are required to keep dry grub in good condition and should be of waterproof construction. For bacon and other meat, I recommend a neoprene bag with zipper-fastened opening. One weighing $2\frac{1}{2}$ ounces will hold 2 or 3 pounds. For other stuff (including the toilet paper) nothing is better than the waxed cloth bags sold by most outfitters. These come in various sizes, those of 5- and 10-pound capacity being about right for bulky items, such as flour, and those of 2-pound capacity for sugar, tea, and so on. Weights and sizes run as follows:

1 pound (one pint)	size	¾ ounce
2 pounds (one quart)	size	1 ounce
5 pounds (two quarts)	size	2 ounces
10 pounds (five quarts)	size	2½ ounces
15 pounds (seven quarts)	size	4 ounces

DUFFEL BAGS should be of good quality, with water-proof throat pieces. I like to put my bedding in an especially good bag, so that it will have a chance to stay dry, even if dropped in the lake.

It is a good thing to stencil an identifying mark on the bottom and side of each bag.

Canoe thwarts are generally about 36 inches apart, which is a good thing to remember when figuring duffel-bag dimensions. Long bags are difficult to get in and out of canoes.

A TUMPLINE of pliable leather is favored by many for toting heavy duffel over portages. The long thongs may be tied around a bundle of any shape and the absence of shoulder straps enables one to slip out from under the load in case of a fall. Of course, the tumpline puts quite a strain on the neck and the strap over the forehead can be very galling on a long, hot portage.

You may find a PACK HARNESS more desirable, as it is true that loaded duffel bags are more easily shaped into a pack with this device. There are very light pack harnesses made of webbing, but their straps have a tendency to slip out of adjustment and I prefer the leather ones, which weigh about 1¼ pounds.

A PACK BOARD is probably the most practical rig of all for heavy carrying. It makes the load rigid and prevents lumps and corners from gouging the back. Ordinarily, the pack board has three crosspieces, to which may be lashed almost any manner of bundle. Some come equipped with packsack, which, of course, limits the bulk of burden to some extent. Weights run from 2¾ pounds, for a board with carrying straps, to 5 or 6 pounds for an outfit complete with sack. Any pack should be carried high on the shoulders.

ROPE is a fairly essential item for any camper. The ³⁄₁₆-inch size, in good Manila, is strong enough for pack lash-

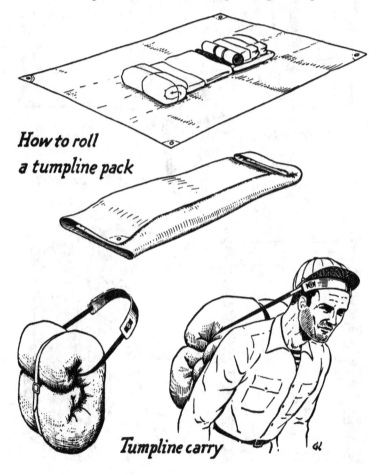

How to roll a tumpline pack

Tumpline carry

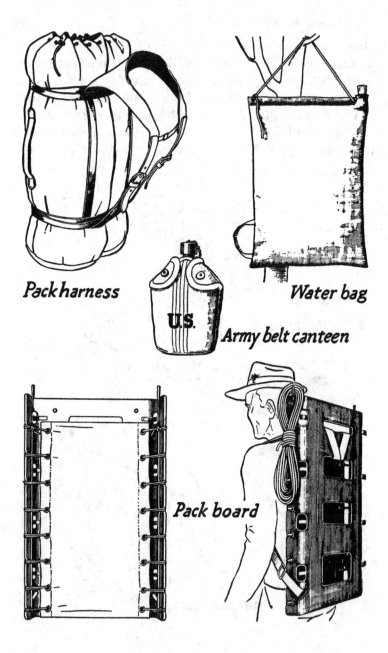

Pack harness

Water bag

Army belt canteen

Pack board

ing, tent guys or anchor line and 50 feet of it, in two pieces, takes up little room. You'll need it for wash line, too. Fifty feet of $\frac{3}{16}$-inch Manila weighs about 11 ounces.

Conveniences

A CANVAS BUCKET is handy for water supply in camp, especially when the main source is at a distance. Get the model without a wire ring around the lip — it will pack easier. Weight, 4 ounces.

A CANVAS WASHBASIN, of the same construction as your bucket, will be a pleasing convenience. If you are finicky, you may use one surface for toilet and the other for laundry, although some woodsmen have been known to wash socks, mix dough and soak beans in the same vessel, without thought of such nicety.

A WATER BAG, of heavy porous material, is a great comfort when water has to be carried, or boiled and stored. The bag's construction allows some seepage from the inside, which, in the course of evaporation, cools the contents. The 2½-gallon size will generously supply two men's needs for a day. Weight, 12 ounces.

A WHISK BROOM is the handiest thing imaginable, for cleaning a tent with sewed-in floor. Ordinary ones weigh about 3 ounces.

FOLDING COTS have been omitted from all but one of my packing lists, for the reason that they are too heavy for consideration when weight is important. They afford extra comfort in some circumstances, however. If you can carry them conveniently, by all means do so, as it is far better to sleep off the ground than on it. The common canvas cot, made 27 inches wide, leaves something to be desired. The 36-inch model, which may be found in completely stocked stores, provides a great deal more comfort and is well worth its extra cost. It is at its best when equipped with an air mattress or pad, as the taut canvas is far from soft and affords but slight protection against chilly drafts underneath. The six legs of a folding cot can be pretty rough on a tent floor and might well be fitted with rubber crutch tips. The 36-inch model mentioned weighs about 21 pounds.

BUG REPELLENT is a must for summer camping. The tightest tent will be invaded by some pests and murder should be their reward. A spray gun of substantial construction is not too difficult to carry, with a supply of liquid insecticide in a screw-top can. If you want something more portable, get a supply of burning powder which is put up in sticks or cones. This latter item is dandy when you are taking a bath, if you can get the smoke to blow around your bare carcass. For protection of your face, neck and hands, take along some liquid or paste bug repellent already proved safe for use on your skin. There will be times, however, when nothing but bobbinet head net and gloves will keep off the more persistent critters.

During World War II, our armed forces used a solution of dimethyl phthalate and water on clothing, to repel insects of all kinds. It is said to be especially effective against chiggers, the bane of our southern woods. A commercial derivative known as "6–12" is available and certainly worth a trial. Don't let it come in contact with rayon or nylon fabric, which it will dissolve.

DDT is a well-known bug repellent, very effective against many insect pests, but somewhat dangerous to humans. I do not recommend it for use on the skin or for a spray in close quarters, such as a tent.

As this is written, vast stores of surplus matériel and equipment are being offered for sale by our Armed Forces.

Many prospective campers will be inclined to seek "bargain" outfits among the retailers of "army goods" and it seems timely to offer a bit of advice on the subject.

Military equipment, in general, is designed for rough

usage by inexperienced and sometimes careless men. For that reason, many of the items are excessively durable and not completely adaptable to a sportsman's use. Consider blankets, as an example. The standard army blanket is woven hard and tight, to afford maximum wear, and thus lacks something in warmth and comfort. Also, it is of minimum size, to conserve weight and space, and is hardly ample to wrap around a big man. I have used army blankets in the past, because I couldn't afford anything better, but switched promptly to bigger, softer covers at the very first opportunity. Perhaps circumstances will govern your initial purchase also, but if you can, invest your outfitting money in commercial merchandise rather than something less satisfactory.

Tents, mess kits and duffel bags fall in the same category. Their low price may not compensate the extra weight and inconvenience they afford.

More than likely, there will be many items of clothing and light equipment among the military surpluses quite suitable for use in the woods. These should be recognizable from the recommendations in my text.

The same cannot be said of canned food items. Many of these will be of the "emergency ration" type and far from completely palatable. Before you decide to stock up on Uncle Sam's version of canned ham and eggs, for instance, ask some G.I. what he thinks of them, or, better yet, get one can and sample it.

Don't expect too much in the way of evolution of camping equipment. The principles of shelter, rest and sustenance are age-old and change but little in the course of time. The outfit you buy today will be entirely satisfactory twenty years hence, if carefully chosen. Materials may be subject to some improvement, especially as to reduction of weight, but I doubt the probability of any development likely to make our present equipment entirely obsolete.

IV

MISCELLANEOUS KITS

TOILET KIT FOR TWO MEN

	Ounces
2 towels, different colors	5
2 combs, different colors	1
2 toothbrushes, different colors (in tubes)	1
1 razor and 5 razor blades	2
1 metal mirror	2
1 tube shaving cream (10-cent size)	1
1 tube tooth paste (10-cent size)	1
1 cake soap, in box	3
	1 pound, 0 ounces

Roll up in towel and secure with large rubber band.

For lighter packing the razor, blades, mirror and shaving cream could be eliminated, saving 5 ounces.

FIRST–AID KIT FOR EXTENDED CAMPING

	Ounces
1 package sodium bicarbonate (baking soda)	5
Cathartic pills, in small bottle	1½
2 small vials New Skin (collodion)	1½
1 small tube Unguentine	1½
½-ounce bottle of 2 per cent tincture of iodine	2
1 package boric acid powder	3

	Ounces
5 yards of 1-inch adhesive tape	2
20 yards of 2-inch gauze bandage	2½
12 gauze pads, 3 × 3 inches	2
36 Readi bandages (assorted sizes)	2
1 razor blade (Gem type, with solid back)	
1 pair tweezers (with sharp points, for slivers, etc.)	½
6 small safety pins	
1 small pair scissors	1
1 Compak snake-bite kit (a spare)	1½
Kit bag for all of above	10

2 pounds, 4 ounces

FIRST–AID KIT FOR SHORT TRIPS

	Ounces
6 sterile gauze pads, 3 × 3 inches	1
10 yards of 2-inch sterile gauze bandage	1¼
2½ yards of 1-inch adhesive tape	1½
1 vial New Skin	¾
1 vial iodine, Mercurochrome, metaphen, or similar germicide	2
12 Readi bandages	½
Unguentine, Carofax or other burn ointment	2
A few cathartic pills in waxed paper	½
Boric acid powder in a plastic tube	1
Leather case or box, for above	3½

14 ounces

FIRST–AID KIT FOR LIGHT PACKING

A tiny little kit, made up about as follows, will suffice for ordinary trips and carry neatly in a small tin box about 4″ × 2½″ × 1″, with a total weight of less than 5 ounces:

2 sterile gauze pads
5 yards of 1-inch gauze bandage

1 vial of Mercurochrome or metaphen
6 finger bandages
1 vial of New Skin
2 ten-cent tubes of Unguentine or Carofax
1 tube of Borofax, yellow oxide or ophthalmic ointment
5 yards of ½-inch adhesive tape

The Boy Scout and Tabloid kits are similar and can be reshuffled a bit to suit individual requirements.

REPAIR KIT FOR CANOE TRIPS

	Ounces
Bag, of 10-ounce canvas, to be ripped apart for patches	1½
File, 4- or 5-inch	½
Whetstone, pocket size	1
Screw driver ⎫ Reel tool ⎭	½
Can of Jeffrey's canoe glue	5½
Small section of cedar canoe plank, 3 × 6 inches	½
⅓ candle, for melting canoe glue	½
Plastic tube, containing:	

    Rubber patches and cement, for mattress repair
    Ferrule cement, for rod repair
    2 rod tip guides
    3 other guides
    4 buttons
    2 needles
    Button thread on card
    Darning cotton on card
    6 split rivets, for pack strap repair
    18 small copper tacks, for canoe repair
    12 small brass screws, for canoe repair   <u>3</u>

                                                     13 ounces

V

COMPLETE OUTFITS

Packing

Put your outfit together in such a way as to afford the most convenience and efficiency. For instance: consider that ponchos, fishing tackle, first-aid kit and camera may be required on a moment's notice and pack them accordingly. Next in accessibility should be the cook kit, which will be needed three times a day.

Your bedding and spare clothing will usually be the last things in demand and so should be packed for undisturbed transport. I always roll mine together and pack in a bag separate from all other equipment. The center of a bedding roll is the safest place to carry jointed fishing rods when shifting camp. It is not at all inconvenient to slip them in or out, as required.

The tent is a once-a-day item, which properly belongs near the bottom of one duffel bag. If you pack it with the cook kit or other miscellaneous hardware, nothing will be harmed by its occasional dampness. That is, nothing but the tent, which should not be rolled up wet, except in emergency and then for the shortest possible time.

You will note that my packing list divides the burden of equipment in fairly even shares: This is important in consideration of portaging and trimming canoes.

The handiest and most practical camping outfit is one designed for two persons. The individual items are compact and easily handled, while units of greater capacity are almost certain to present problems in transport and management. A big tent, for example, requires lots of labor and skill for erection and, once filled with people, it will never seem quite large enough to contain all the personalities and impedimenta. A shelter for two, on the other hand, may be quickly set up and a pair of partners will invariably work out better arrangements than a larger group.

The flexibility of operations made possible with a two-person outfit is most desirable. Two can come to an agreement and get started while four are warming up to a debate, and yet there is nothing to prevent them from joining a party and sharing the fun of community endeavor.

Your own imagination will disclose many other advantages to be found in a twosome program, so I'll dwell no longer on the subject but go on with specifications and suggestions based on that assumption.

Automobile Cruising

Automobile cruising, or motor camping, is most attractive to prosperous folk who want outdoor life without too much of the primitive. I say "prosperous," because the comforts of home are fairly expensive, when carried afield.

There follows a list of items convenient and practical for the motorized camper. They will, perforce, limit his activity to fairly tame country, where roadside camp sites are available and back-packing is out of the picture, but they surely will provide comfort.

The list is quite elaborate, simply to illustrate the possibilities. Anyone can trim it to suit personal limitations, or fill it out with icebox, radio and croquet set, so far as I am concerned.

Food to complement such an outfit presents no problem. Everything imaginable can be found in cans and menus worked out with reckless disregard for weight. You might use my two-weeks grub list for a guide, substituting canned goods for most of the staples, and arrive at a pretty efficient culinary program. I don't believe any greater detail is necessary, in this particular bracket.

PACKING LIST FOR AUTOMOBILE CRUISING

	Pounds	Ounces
Tent, umbrella or wall model, 9′ × 9′ or 10′ × 10′, complete with stakes, frame, etc.	60	0
Tarpaulin, for dining fly	6	8
2 cots, folding canvas, 36″ wide	41	8
2 air mattresses, 32″ × 75″	16	0
Pump for mattresses	1	0
2 pillows	2	8
6 blankets, 4 pounds each	24	0
2 armchairs, folding canvas	25	0
2 stools, folding canvas	6	8
1 table, folding	15	0
2 sets of shelves, folding canvas	9	0
Spare clothing and footwear	27	0
Cookstove, gasoline, with oven	20	0
Stand for stove, folding	2	0
Cook kit	9	6
2 water bags, 2½-gallon	1	8
2 buckets, canvas	1	0
Broom	1	8
Hand ax	2	4
Shovel	3	4

	Pounds	Ounces
Lantern, gasoline	5	0
Repair kit	1	3
Spray gun and insecticide	1	8
Rope, four 25' pieces 1/4" Manila	1	8
Clothespins		8
First-aid kit	2	5
2 washbasins, canvas		14
6 towels	1	8
2 toilet kits	2	0
Bathtub, canvas	1	8
Toilet tent	4	8
Toilet seat, folding, with paper bags	8	0
Toilet paper — 1000 sheets — in water-proof bag		12
Flashlight		12
600 matches, in 2 waterproof cans		10
Bug repellent — 2 bottles		12
200 Halazone tablets		3
2 ponchos or raincoats	3	
Fishing tackle	10	
2 rods	2	
2 landing nets	1	8
Minnow seine	1	5
Minnow bucket	2	0
Cameras and film	4	
Playing cards		6
Cigarettes or tobacco and spare pipe	2	8
Gasoline, 5 gallons in gallon cans	40	
Food for 2 weeks	110	
2 duffel bags, 15" × 36", for bedding and clothing	4	4
2 duffel bags, 12" × 36", for tools, kits and miscellany	3	0
2 wooden boxes, with hinged lids, for the food supply	7	12
Approximate total weight of outfit	500	0

If the weight and expense of this list scare you, or you want something more portable, whittle it down. For permanent camping beside some favorite lake or stream,

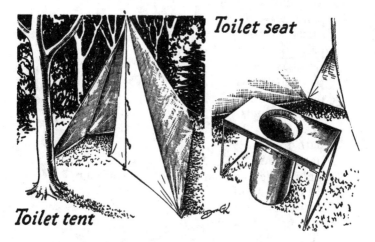

Toilet seat

Toilet tent

reasonably remote from the highway, you could be mighty comfortable with an assortment of equipment on the order of the following:

Portable Outfit for
Two Weeks of Mild Weather
256 Pounds, 7 Ounces

Gather together the necessary items:

    1 tent, Explorer, 8′ × 8′ (Aberlite)
    17 aluminum tent stakes
    1 tent pole and ridge, collapsible
    1 gasoline stove, 2-burner
    2 folding camp stools

1 folding table (short-legged)
4 blankets, 4 pounds each
2 air mattresses, 25″ × 75″
2 air pillows
4 pairs drawers
4 shirts (cotton pull-overs)
2 pairs pants
2 sweaters
4 pairs socks, wool
2 pairs moccasins
4 handkerchiefs
2 head nets
2 bath towels
2 hand towels
Supply of cigarettes or tobacco for two men
2 fly rods, in tubes
Camera and film
2 ponchos, neoprene
Fishing tackle
2 landing nets, folding
First-aid kit
Repair kit
Toilet kit
Cook kit
1 water bag, Desert, 2½-gallon
1 bucket, canvas
1 washbasin, canvas
Pump for air mattresses
Spray gun for insecticide
Can of insecticide
Whisk broom
Toilet paper, 1000 sheets
200 Halazone tablets
1 flashlight and batteries
4 candles, in cardboard box
600 matches, waterproofed
2 bottles bug repellent

1 strainer funnel, for filling stove
Rope, two 25' pieces of $\frac{3}{16}$" Manila
Hand ax, in sheath
Trench shovel, in sheath
Breadboard of plywood, 12" × 18"
2 two-gallon canteens of gasoline
1 pack board
Pack cloth, 7' × 8'
2 pack harnesses or tumplines
1 butter can, aluminum
2 friction-top cans for matches
1 friction-top can for grease
4 duffel bags, 12" × 36" (drawstring top)
2 duffel bags, 12" × 24" (zipper side openings)
2 bags for clothing
2 shoe bags for moccasins
2 shoe bags for fishing tackle
1 shoe bag for tent stakes
1 bag for cook kit
1 bag for miscellany
2 bacon bags, neoprene
2 waterproof 1-pound food bags
7 waterproof 2-pound food bags
12 waterproof 5-pound food bags
2 waterproof 15-pound food bags
   Food as outlined in grocery list for two weeks of
   cruising

and pack them in accordance with the outline following:

BAG NUMBER ONE

	Pounds	Ounces
Duffel bag, 12″ × 36″	1	8
2 wool blankets, 4 pounds each	8	0
Air mattress	6	0
Air pillow		6
Pump for mattress		12

Spare clothing:	Ounces		
2 towels (1 bath, 1 hand)	8		
2 pairs drawers	14		
2 shirts	15		
Pants	24		
Sweater	9		
2 pairs socks	6		
Moccasins, in separate bag	21		
2 handkerchiefs	2		
Head net	1		
Bag	4	6	8
Cigarettes or spare pipe and tobacco		1	0
Fly rod, in tube		1	0
Pack strap or tumpline		1	4
		26	6

BAG NUMBER TWO

	Pounds	Ounces
Duffel bag, 12" × 36"	1	8
2 wool blankets, 4 pounds each	8	0
Air mattress	6	0
Air pillow		6
Insecticide, in screw-top can		10
Spray gun, for same		6

Spare clothing:	Ounces		
2 towels (1 bath, 1 hand)	8		
2 pairs drawers	14		
2 shirts	15		
Pants	24		
Sweater	9		
2 pairs socks	6		
Moccasins, in separate bag	21		
2 handkerchiefs	2		
Head net	1		
Bag	4	6	8
Cigarettes or spare pipe and tobacco		1	0
Fly rod, in tube		1	0
Pack strap or tumpline		1	4
		26	10

BAG NUMBER THREE

	Pounds	Ounces
Duffel bag, 12" × 36"	1	8
Whisk broom		3
17 tent stakes, aluminum, in bag	2	0
Tent, Explorer, 8' × 8' (Aberlite)	15	8

Bag of miscellany, containing:	Ounces		
First-aid kit	14		
Repair kit	13		
Toilet kit	16		
Washbasin, canvas	4		
Toilet paper, 1000 sheets, in waterproof bag	12		
200 Halazone tablets	3		
Flashlight and spare batteries	9		
4 candles, in a cardboard box	7		
600 waterproofed matches, in 2 cans	10		
Bug repellent, 2 bottles	12		
Films for camera	4		
Strainer funnel, for filling stove	3		
Bag, for all of above	5	7	0
		26	3

BAG NUMBER FOUR

	Pounds	Ounces
Duffel bag, 12" × 36"	1	8
Rope, two 25' pieces of ³⁄₁₆" Manila		11
Bucket, canvas		4
Cook kit	9	6
Water bag, desert, 2½-gallon		12
Hand ax, in sheath	2	4
Trench shovel, in sheath	1	15
2 folding landing nets	1	0
2 bags of fly-fishing tackle	3	0
Camera, in leather case	2	0
2 ponchos	2	0
	24	12

PACK

	Pounds	Ounces
Pack cloth, 7' × 8', for dining fly	3	8
Pack board	2	12
Tent pole and ridge, collapsible	4	2
Two-burner gasoline stove, with folding oven	20	0
Breadboard, plywood, 12" × 18"	1	0
	31	6

ODDS AND ENDS

	Pounds	Ounces
2 canteens of gasoline, 2-gallon	29	10
2 folding camp stools	5	0
Folding table (stools carry inside it)	6	8
	41	2

	Pounds	Ounces
Food, in two zipper bags	80	0

All of the foregoing adds up to the impressive total of 256 pounds 7 ounces, and comes pretty close to being the kind of outfit which includes "everything that might come in handy."

It can be carried in an 18-foot canoe, with two big men, but they will grunt under the burden if many long portages are encountered. It is really portable, however, as no single package weighs much over 40 pounds.

The bags of personal stuff will tote nicely with the pack harness included, but the camp gear and food packs require the pack board, if comfort is any consideration.

A summary of the bundles follows:

	Pounds	Ounces
Bag No. 1	26	6
Bag No. 2	26	10
Bag No. 3	26	3
Bag No. 4	24	12
Pack	31	6
Odds and ends	41	2
Food, in two bags	80	0
	256	7

You'll note that the packing list, so far, puts each man's personal stuff in a separate bag and splits the general equipment into two small packages of nearly equal size and weight. This affords several little advantages not to be scorned. For one, there is less chance of damaging or losing all the blankets and clothing in an accident and the individual bags make decent loads for back-packing. Further, the two bags can be used to sit on.

A Comfortable Outfit for
a Week's Canoe Trip
135 Pounds, 7 Ounces

A canoe trip presents a good run-of-the-mine problem in light outfitting; let us put together some equipment and see how it shapes up for that purpose. There are a few factors to be considered before we begin, however.

First, there is the matter of portability. Long portages may be encountered and we will want to get over them with a minimum of toil and sweat. We may also find some of our camp sites on high banks and be required to heave the outfit up and over. For such reasons our various bags and bundles must be light enough to handle easily and without danger of accident.

Next comes the business of navigation. A canoe must be safely loaded and properly trimmed, to the end that our outfit cannot be too heavy or unwieldy. It must also be protected from a possible ducking or drenching, so that we may sleep in dry blankets and eat wholesome grub, at least most of the time.

We must anticipate a general scarcity of good firewood, pure drinking water and tent poles, for there are few canoe trails where these items are now plentiful.

We should prepare with the idea of experiencing pleasure, rather than a test of endurance, and take what is necessary to our comfort and recreation.

That may appear to be quite a bill of goods, but it's feasible enough, when you get into the details. You may and probably will make changes in my lists to suit your own circumstances or desires, but in general they afford a pretty good outline of what is needed to meet present-day conditions.

Equip with the best you can afford, with regard for the possibility of an occasional beating from the elements. Water-soaked bedding and wind-torn tents can bring plenty of distress to the toughest of *voyageurs* and no amount of skill or caution can offset the weaknesses of shoddy materials. The duffel bags for your bedding, in particular, should be as waterproof as possible; not only for protection from rain, but from bilge water as well. The tightest canoe may ship considerable water at times, and a half inch of it, sloshing around in the bilge, will soon soak through any but a good bag.

Anyhow, assemble the articles next listed:

1 tent, Cruiser, 5′ × 7′ (Aberlite)
Tent pole and ridge, collapsible
Pocket stove and container
4 blankets, 4 pounds each
2 air mattresses, 25″ × 75″
2 pairs drawers
2 pairs socks
2 sweaters
4 handkerchiefs
2 head nets
Supply of cigarettes or tobacco for two men
2 fly rods, in tubes
Camera and film
2 ponchos, neoprene
Fishing tackle
2 landing nets, folding
Razor, blades and shaving cream
2 toothbrushes
1 tube toothpaste, small
2 combs
1 small cake of soap

1 plastic soap box
2 towels
Small first-aid kit
Repair kit
1 frying pan, aluminum, 8½-inch
1 coffeepot, aluminum, 2-quart
2 plates, aluminum
2 cups, enamelware
2 spoons
2 forks
2 knives
1 spatula
1 can opener
1 salt shaker
1 dish towel
1 dishcloth
6 soap pads
1 water bag, Desert, 2½-gallon
Pump for air mattresses
Toilet paper, 500 sheets
100 Halazone tablets
Flashlight and batteries
300 matches, waterproofed
1 bottle bug repellent
2 bootlaces, 60 inches, leather
Rope, two 25′ pieces of ³⁄₁₆″ Manila
1 hand ax, in sheath
2 canteens of gasoline, 2-quart
1 pack board
2 pack harnesses
1 butter can, aluminum
1 friction-top can for matches
1 friction-top can for grease
3 duffel bags, 12″ × 36″ (drawstring top)
2 duffel bags, 9″ × 24″ (drawstring top)
2 bags for clothing
2 shoe bags for fishing tackle

1 bag for cook kit
1 bag for miscellany
1 bacon bag, neoprene
3 waterproof 1-pound food bags
4 waterproof 2-pound food bags
7 waterproof 5-pound food bags
2 waterproof 15-pound food bags
Flour sack for half of grub
Food as listed under grocery list for one week of cruising

and pack according to following outline:

BAG NUMBER ONE

	Pounds	Ounces
Waterproof duffel bag, 12″ × 36″	1	8
2 wool blankets, 72″ × 84″, 4 pounds each	8	0
Air mattress, 25″ × 75″	6	0

Spare clothing, in drawstring bag:	Ounces		
Pair of drawers	7		
Pair of socks	3		
Sweater	9		
2 handkerchiefs	2		
Bag	4	1	9
Camera and films		2	4
Cigarettes or spare pipe and tobacco			7
Fly-fishing tackle, in bag		1	8
Folding landing net			8
Fly rod, in tube		1	0
Poncho		1	0
Pack harness		1	4
		25	0

BAG NUMBER TWO

	Pounds	Ounces
Waterproof duffel bag, 12" × 36"	1	8
2 wool blankets, 72" × 84", 4 pounds each	8	0
Air mattress, 25" × 75"	6	0
Pump for air mattress		12

Spare clothing, in drawstring bag: *Ounces*

	Ounces	Pounds	Ounces
Pair of drawers	7		
Pair of socks	3		
Sweater	9		
2 handkerchiefs	2		
Bag	4	1	9

Toilet kit:

	Ounces	Pounds	Ounces
Razor, blades and shaving cream	3		
2 toothbrushes	1		
Tube of tooth paste	1		
2 combs	1		
Cake of soap in a box	3		
2 towels, different colors	5		14
Cigarettes or spare pipe and tobacco			7
Fly-fishing tackle, in bag		1	8
Folding landing net			8
Fly rod, in tube		1	0
Poncho		1	0
Pack harness		1	4
		24	6

BAG NUMBER THREE

	Pounds	Ounces
Duffel bag, 9″ × 24″	1	0
Tent, Cruiser, 5′ × 7′	7	8
Tent pole and ridge, steel	1	6

Bag of miscellany, as follows:	Ounces		
First-aid kit	5		
Repair kit	13		
Toilet paper, 500 sheets, in water-proof bag	6		
Flashlight	3		
300 waterproofed matches, in friction-top can	4½		
1 bottle bug repellent	6		
2 head nets	2		
100 Halazone tablets	1½		
2 leather bootlaces, about 60 inches long	5		
Bag	5	3	3
Rope, two 25′ pieces of ³⁄₁₆″ Manila			11
Hand ax, in sheath		1	8
		15	4

BAG NUMBER FOUR

	Ounces	Pounds	Ounces
Duffel bag, 9" × 24"		1	0
Cook kit:			
1 frying pan, aluminum, 8½-inch	12		
1 coffeepot, aluminum, 2-quart	13		
2 plates, aluminum	6		
2 cups, enamelware	6		
2 spoons	4		
2 forks	3		
2 knives	4		
1 spatula	4		
1 can opener	2		
1 salt shaker	1		
1 dish towel	3		
1 dishcloth	2		
6 soap pads, for dishwashing	2		
Empty friction-top can, for grease	3		
Bag	4	4	5
"Pocket" stove and container, 4½" × 8½". (The two parts of the container serve as pot and mixing pan.)		2	12
1 gallon of gasoline, in two 2-quart canteens (one week's supply of fuel)		9	0
		17	1

Food to feed two men amply for a week, including all the necessary containers and a duffel bag, will weigh 39 pounds, as detailed in a succeeding chapter.

A supply of drinking water may be a necessity and 1 gallon in a water bag will add about 9 pounds to the outfit.

Two paddles will probably total 3 pounds in weight.

So, if you are equipped as suggested to travel in a standard 18-foot canoe, your transport problem will appear as follows:

	Pounds	Ounces
Bag No. 1	25	0
Bag No. 2	24	6
Bag No. 3	15	4
Bag No. 4	17	1
Grub sack	39	0
Pack board	2	12
Filled water bag	9	0
2 paddles	3	0
Total weight of outfit	135	7
Canoe	85	0

On a portage

Two reasonably husky men can hike all this freight over any but the toughest portages in two trips, on something like the following basis:

	Pounds	Ounces
FIRST TRIP:		
One man carrying the canoe and paddles	88	0
The other carrying the pack board, with		
Bag No. 3, Bag No. 4 and the grub sack	74	1
SECOND TRIP:		
One man carrying Bag No. 1	25	0
The other carrying Bag No. 2 and the		
water bag	33	6

If the men aren't so husky, or prefer lighter toil, they may split up the burden and make three easy trips, in some such order as:

	Pounds	Ounces
FIRST TRIP:		
Both men carrying the canoe	85	0
SECOND TRIP:		
One man carrying the pack board with the grub sack	41	12
The other carrying Bag No. 1 and Bag No. 3	40	4
THIRD TRIP:		
One man carrying Bag No. 2 and the paddles	27	6
The other carrying Bag No. 4 and the water bag	26	1

Thus no back is broken and the loads are equitably divided. Of course, some of the weights change every day, as food and fuel are consumed and the water supply varies, but the small parcels afford enough flexibility to equalize loads, nevertheless.

Make no mistake about it — this is a heavy load for a small canoe. If you expect to encounter fast rivers and big lakes, play safe with a big canoe; preferably the 18-foot Guides model.

If you persist in roughing it, or feel certain that supplies of drinking water, firewood and browse will be available every day, you may strip down to essentials and assemble an outfit to carry safely in a 15-foot canoe weighing as little as 45 pounds. Such tiny craft are apt to be cranky in heavy water, however, and you'll find most experienced *voyageurs* using the standard 18-foot Guides model in preference to anything smaller.

With an outfit such as that next itemized, and an 85-

pound canoe, two healthy men can make every portage in one trip. They might thus save enough time and labor every day to offset the chore of making browse beds and cooking fires. Anyhow, here goes for lighter weights.

Light Outfit for
a Week's Canoe Trip
97 Pounds, 7 Ounces

The items:

1 tent, Cruiser, 5′ × 7′ (Aberlite)
4 blankets, 4 pounds each
2 pairs drawers
2 pairs socks, wool
2 sweaters
4 handkerchiefs
2 head nets
Supply of cigarettes or tobacco for two men
2 fly rods, in tubes
Camera and films
2 ponchos, neoprene
Fishing tackle
Razor, blades and shaving cream
2 toothbrushes
1 tube tooth paste, small
2 combs
1 small cake of soap
2 towels
Small first-aid kit
Repair kit
1 frying pan, aluminum, 8½-inch
1 pot, aluminum, 3¼-quart

1 coffeepot, aluminum, 2-quart
1 mixing pan, aluminum, 1¾-quart
2 plates, aluminum
2 cups, Beetleware
2 spoons
2 forks
Spatula blade to fit on fork
1 can opener
1 dish towel
6 soap pads
Toilet paper, 500 sheets
100 Halazone tablets
Flashlight and battery
300 matches, waterproofed
1 bottle bug repellent
2 bootlaces, 60 inches, leather
Rope, two 25' pieces of ³⁄₁₆" Manila
1 hand ax, in sheath
1 pack board
1 tumpline
1 butter can, aluminum
1 friction-top can for matches
1 friction-top can for grease
4 duffel bags, 12" × 36" (drawstring top)
2 shoe bags for fishing tackle
1 bag for cook kit
1 bag for miscellany
1 bag for bacon, neoprene
3 waterproof 1-pound food bags
4 waterproof 2-pound food bags
7 waterproof 5-pound food bags
2 waterproof 15-pound food bags
1 flour sack for half of grub
1 neoprene tobacco pouch, for soap
    Food as listed under grocery list for one week of cruising.

    The packing outline follows:

BAG NUMBER ONE

		Pounds	Ounces
Duffel bag, 12″ × 36″		1	8
2 wool blankets, 72″ × 84″, 4 pounds each		8	o
Spare clothing, rolled in the towel:	*Ounces*		
Pair of drawers	7		
Pair of socks	2½		
Sweater	8		
2 handkerchiefs	2		
Towel	2½	1	6
Cigarettes or spare pipe and tobacco		o	7
Camera and films		2	4
Fly-fishing tackle		1	8
Fly rod, in tube		1	o
Poncho		1	o
		17	1

BAG NUMBER TWO

		Pounds	Ounces
Duffel bag, 12″ × 36″		1	8
2 wool blankets, 72″ × 84″, 4 pounds each		8	o
Spare clothing, rolled in the towel:	*Ounces*		
Pair of drawers	7		
Pair of socks	2½		
Sweater	8		
2 handkerchiefs	2		
Towel	2½	1	6
Toilet kit:	*Ounces*		
Razor, blades and shaving cream	3		
2 toothbrushes	1		
Tube of tooth paste	1		
2 combs	1		
Cake of soap, in bag	2	o	8
Cigarettes or spare pipe and tobacco		o	7
Fly-fishing tackle, in bag		1	8
Fly rod, in tube		1	o
Poncho		1	o
Tumpline		1	4
		16	9

BAG NUMBER THREE

	Pounds	Ounces
Duffel bag, 12" × 36"	1	8
Tent, Cruiser, 5' × 7'	7	8

Bag of miscellany:

	Ounces		
First-aid kit	5		
Repair kit	13		
Toilet paper, 500 sheets in waterproof bag	6		
Flashlight	3		
Spare battery	1		
300 waterproofed matches, in can	4½		
Bottle of bug repellent	6		
2 head nets	2		
100 Halazone tablets	1½		
2 leather bootlaces, 60-inch	5		
Bag	4	3	3
Rope, two 25' pieces of 3⁄16" Manila		0	11
Hand ax, in sheath		1	8

Cook kit:

	Ounces		
Frying pan, 8½-inch, aluminum	12		
Pot, 3¼-quart, aluminum	13		
Coffeepot, aluminum	13		
Mixing pan, 1¾-quart, aluminum	7		
2 plates, aluminum	6		
2 cups, Beetleware	3		
2 spoons	2		
2 forks	3		
Spatula blade, to fit fork	1		
Dish towel	3		
6 soap pads, for dishwashing	2		
Empty can, for grease	3		
Can opener	2		
Bag, for all of above	5	4	11
		19	1

A summary of individual packages follows:

	Pounds	Ounces
Bag No. 1	17	1
Bag No. 2	16	9
Bag No. 3	19	1
Grub pack	39	0
Pack board	2	12
Paddles	3	0
Total weight of outfit	97	7
Canoe	85	0

Portaging could be accomplished quite simply by:

One man carrying the canoe and paddles	88	0
His partner carrying all the other equipment	94	7

Or, if desired, two trips could be made:

FIRST TRIP:

Both men carrying the canoe	85	0

SECOND TRIP:

One man carrying the pack board, with grub pack and paddles	44	12
The other carrying bags Nos. 1, 2 and 3, with the tumpline	52	11

Outfitting for a Two Weeks' Canoe Trip
158 Pounds, 12 Ounces

An outfit for two weeks of canoe travel can run into a lot of weight and cause plenty of weariness on portages, if you equip recklessly.

As an example, take the "comfortable" outfit for a week's canoe trip and add: 40 pounds of food, a gallon of fuel, baking equipment and a couple of pounds of miscellaneous supplies. You'll find yourself with a burden of 190 pounds, exclusive of the canoe! Make a few long carries with that and you'll begin to wonder why you left home.

If you expect to spend your two weeks in country where firewood, drinking water and tent poles may be scarce, take along the substitutes and plan to hunt up a grocery store at the end of the first week. More than likely there will be one somewhere within walking distance of your waterway. If not, it might be possible to have a package of replenishments sent in to a resident of the country. There will be some permanent establishment in any well-traveled territory, you may be sure.

Let us assume, however, that a two weeks' trip is to be planned for exploration of real wilderness. In such case, you may eliminate the stove and fuel, the water bag, tent pole and stakes, with a consequent reduction in weight of 25 pounds or more. I'd suggest that you take air mattresses and pump on any two weeks' trip, as you will surely tire of browse beds in that time.

So, let us again shuffle the duffel and see what comes of it.

You will require:

1 tent, Cruiser, 5' × 7' (Aberlite)
4 blankets, 4 pounds each
2 air mattresses, 25" × 75"
2 pairs drawers
4 pairs socks, wool
2 sweaters
4 handkerchiefs
2 head nets
Supply of cigarettes or tobacco for two men
2 fly rods, in tubes
Camera and films
2 ponchos, neoprene

Fishing tackle
2 bath towels
2 hand towels
Razor, blades and shaving cream
2 tooth brushes
1 tube toothpaste, small
2 combs
1 cake of toilet soap
½ cake of laundry soap and 4 clothespins
First-aid kit
Repair kit
1 frying pan, aluminum, 8½-inch
1 coffeepot, aluminum, 2-quart
1 pot, aluminum, 3¼-quart
1 reflector oven, aluminum
1 mixing pan, aluminum, 1¾-quart
2 plates, aluminum
2 cups, Beetleware
2 spoons
2 forks
Spatula blade to fit on fork
1 can opener
1 dish towel
12 soap pads
Toilet paper, 1000 sheets
200 Halazone tablets
Flashlight and spare battery
600 matches, waterproofed
2 candles, in cardboard box
2 bottles bug repellent
2 bootlaces, 60 inches, leather
50 feet ³⁄₁₆″ Manila rope
1 hand ax, in sheath
1 pump for air mattress
Breadboard of plywood, 12″ × 18″
1 pack board
1 pack harness

1 butter can, aluminum
2 friction-top cans for matches
1 friction-top can for grease
3 duffel bags, 12″ × 36″ (drawstring top)
2 duffel bags, 12″ × 24″ (zipper side opening)
1 bag for laundry soap and clothespins
2 shoe bags for fishing tackle
1 bag for cook kit
2 bags for bacon, neoprene
1 bag for miscellany
2 waterproof 1-pound food bags
7 waterproof 2-pound food bags
12 waterproof 5-pound food bags
2 waterproof 15-pound food bags
2 neoprene tobacco pouches, for soap
Food as per grocery list for two weeks of cruising.

To be packed as follows:

BAG NUMBER ONE

	Pounds	Ounces
Duffel bag, 12″ × 36″	1	8
Air mattress	6	0
2 wool blankets, 72″ × 84″, 4 pounds each	8	

Spare clothing, rolled in a towel:	*Ounces*		
Pair of drawers	7		
2 pairs of socks	5		
Sweater	8		
2 handkerchiefs	2		
2 towels	5	1	11
Laundry soap and clothespins, in a bag		0	5
Cigarettes or spare pipe and tobacco		0	12
Camera and film		2	4
Fly-fishing tackle, in bag		1	8
Fly rod, in tube		1	0
Poncho		1	0
		24	0

BAG NUMBER TWO

	Pounds	Ounces
Duffel bag, 12" × 36"	1	8
Air mattress	6	0
Pump for air mattresses	0	12
2 wool blankets, 72" × 84", 4 pounds each	8	0

Spare clothing: *Ounces*

	Ounces		
Pair of drawers	7		
2 pairs of socks	5		
Sweater	8		
2 handkerchiefs	2		
2 towels	5	1	11

Toilet kit: *Ounces*

	Ounces		
Razor, blades and shaving cream	3		
2 toothbrushes	1		
Tube of tooth paste	1		
2 combs	1		
Cake of soap, in a bag	2	0	8

	Pounds	Ounces
Cigarettes or spare pipe and tobacco	0	12
Fly-fishing tackle, in bag	1	8
Fly rod, in tube	1	0
Poncho	1	0
Pack harness	1	4
	23	15

BAG NUMBER THREE

	Pounds	Ounces
Duffel bag, 12″ × 36″	1	8
Tent, Cruiser	7	8

Bag of miscellany, containing: *Ounces*

	Ounces		
First-aid kit	14		
Repair kit	13		
Toilet paper, 1000 sheets in water-proof bag	12		
Flashlight	3		
Spare battery	1		
2 candles, in cardboard box	3		
600 waterproofed matches, in two cans	9		
2 bottles of bug repellent	12		
2 head nets	2		
200 Halazone tablets	3		
2 leather bootlaces, 60 inches long	5		
Bag	4	5	1
Rope, 50 feet of ³⁄₁₆″ Manila		0	11
Hand ax, in sheath		1	8

Cook kit: *Ounces*

	Ounces		
Frying pan, aluminum, 8½-inch	12		
Pot, aluminum, 3¼-quart	13		
Coffeepot, aluminum, 2-quart	13		
Mixing pan, aluminum, 1¾-qt.	7		
2 plates	6		
2 cups, Beetleware	3		
2 spoons	2		
2 forks	3		
Spatula blade	1		
Dish towel	3		
12 soap pads, for dishwashing	4		
Empty can, for grease	3		
Can opener	2		
Bag for all of above	5	4	13
		21	1

In summary, the outfit would appear thus:

	Pounds	Ounces
Bag No. 1	24	0
Bag No. 2	23	15
Bag No. 3	21	1
Grub pack	80	0
Breadboard and reflector	4	0
Pack board	2	12
Paddles	3	0
	158	12
Canoe	85	0

The job of portaging would shape up about as follows:

FIRST TRIP:

One man carrying the canoe and paddles	88	0
The other carrying the pack board, with the breadboard, reflector and grub pack	86	12

·SECOND TRIP:

One man carrying the pack board with Bag No. 3	23	13
The other carrying Bag No. 1 and Bag No. 2	47	15

If expedient, one man could carry Bags Nos. 1, 2 and 3 on the pack board the second trip, leaving his partner occupied with the preparation of a meal or some other chore.

Or, if preferred, three easy trips could be made:

	Pounds	Ounces

FIRST TRIP:

Both men carrying the canoe	85	0

SECOND TRIP:

One carrying half the grub, on the pack board	43	2
The other carrying Bags Nos. 1 and 3	45	1

	Pounds	Ounces

THIRD TRIP:

One carrying half the grub, on the pack
board 42   6

The other carrying Bag No. 2, the reflector and breadboard, and the pad-
dles 30   15

Outfit for a Portable Hunting Camp
123 Pounds, 5 Ounces

A hunter's camp, usually located where spruce, balsam, or other good browse is plentiful, may be rigged largely with materials at hand.

Lay two logs, about 8 or 10 inches in diameter and 7 or 8 feet long, parallel to one another; as far apart as the width of your tent. Drive some stakes to keep them from rolling. On the base logs, lay a floor of smooth, springy poles, 2 or 2½ inches in diameter and long enough to overhang the logs a foot or so. Fasten the floor poles in place with 2 cleats, 2 or 3 inches in diameter, laid over the base logs (on top of the floor poles) and spiked down at each end. Spike the outside floor poles to the base logs and the cleats to these, using twentypenny nails. Build your browse bed on the floor and pitch the tent over it, tying the tent-stake loops to nails driven into the floor poles. If your tent has a sewed-in floor; so much the better. If not, a ground cloth should cover the browse.

Browse beds are best when built of small spruce, balsam or cedar branchlets, about the size of your hand, laid on edge. Start the first row against one of the cleats and work back; slapping each newly applied branchlet onto the preceding row, so that it will mat or mesh, as you might say, into a solid mass. The "slapping" is accomplished by a flick of the wrist, with the branchlet held loosely by the fingers.

You'll be surprised by the amount of browse required for a respectable bed and your first attempt at construction may

Hunter's camp and browse bed

not be a total success; perhaps because of the inadequacy of my instructions. You'll soon get the hang of it, however, and be able to do a regular, professional job, about the second try.

Portable Hunting Camp

A very simple outfit may serve well as a portable hunting camp, as conditions to be expected in hunting season and hunting territory are generally favorable to practice of the woodsman's art. For one thing, bugs and snakes will be out of circulation in the north country just as soon as frost is in the air, and provision for their frustration may be eliminated. Firewood and browse will probably be plentiful in country affording game cover, and the cooking and sleeping equipment can be simplified in consequence. The grub list might well be worked out on a scheme similar to that suggested for back-packers, in expectation of an occasional kill for the pot.

Personally, I prefer the hunting season to all others for outdoor living. The forest is at its best then, and the minor annoyances of summer camping are not present. The keen air of autumn adds zest to every activity and affords the finest campfire sitting ever, when the dishes are washed and the last pipe before bedtime completes a day of contentment.

You'll need these articles for a week in the autumn woods:

1 tent, lean-to, 6' × 6⅓' × 5' (Aberlite)
4 heavy wool blankets, 6 pounds each
2 pairs woolen drawers
2 woolen undershirts
4 pairs heavy wool socks
2 sweaters
2 knitted caps
2 pairs moccasins
4 handkerchiefs
4 towels
Supply of cigarettes or tobacco for two men
1 small first-aid kit
Cake of soap, 2 toothbrushes, small tube of tooth paste, 2 combs
1 small file
1 small whetstone
50 feet of chalk line
Filled oiler
Cleaning patches

Pull-through cleaner
Screw driver
24 twentypenny nails
6 buttons
8 split rivets
Needles and button thread
Darning cotton
Plastic tube for buttons, rivets, etc.
100 Halazone tablets
Toilet paper, 500 sheets
Flashlight and battery
2 candles, in cardboard box
300 matches, waterproofed
Fire starter, ½ package
30 rifle cartridges
25 feet of 3⁄16″ Manila rope
1 ax, about 4 pounds
1 pack board
1 tumpline
1 pack cloth, 6′ × 7′
Frying pan, aluminum, 8½-inch
Pot and cover, aluminum, 3¼-quart
Coffeepot, aluminum, 2-quart
Mixing pan, aluminum, 1¾-quart
2 plates, aluminum
2 cups, enamelware
2 spoons
2 forks
2 knives
1 spatula
Salt shaker
Dish towel
Dishcloth
6 soap pads
1 butter can, aluminum
1 friction-top can for matches
1 friction-top can for grease

3 duffel bags, 12" × 36" (drawstring top)
2 bags for clothing
1 bag for bacon, neoprene
1 bag for miscellany
1 bag for cook kit
3 waterproof 1-pound food bags
4 waterproof 2-pound food bags
8 waterproof 5-pound food bags
2 waterproof 15-pound food bags
1 flour sack for part of grub supply
Food as outlined in grocery list for one week of cruising.

Pack them as follows:

BAG NUMBER ONE

	Ounces	Pounds	Ounces
Duffel bag, 12" × 36"		1	8
2 blankets, 72" × 84", 6 pounds each		12	0
Spare clothing:			
1 pair woolen drawers	16		
1 woolen undershirt	12		
2 pairs heavy wool socks	8		
1 pair moccasins	14		
2 handkerchiefs	2		
Sweater	24		
Knitted cap	3		
2 towels	5		
Bag, for above	4	5	8
Cigarettes or spare pipe and tobacco		0	7
		19	7

BAG NUMBER TWO

	Pounds	Ounces
Duffel bag, 12″ × 36″	1	8
2 blankets, 72″ × 84″, 6 pounds each	12	0

Spare clothing:	Ounces		
1 pair woolen drawers	16		
1 woolen undershirt	12		
2 pairs heavy wool socks	8		
1 pair moccasins	14		
2 handkerchiefs	2		
Sweater	24		
Knitted cap	3		
2 towels	5		
Bag, for above	4	5	8
Cigarettes or spare pipe and tobacco		0	7
		19	7

PACK

	Pounds	Ounces
Pack cloth, 6′ × 7′, waterproof (use also as ground cloth)	2	8
Lean-to tent, 6′ × 6⅓′ × 5′	5	0
Rope, 25 feet of ³⁄₁₆″ Manila		6

Bag of miscellany, containing:	Ounces
First-aid kit	5

Repair kit:
File
Whetstone
50 feet chalk line
Filled oiler
Cleaning patches
Pull-through cleaner
Screw driver
24 twentypenny nails

	Ounces	*Pounds*	*Ounces*
Buttons ⎫			
Split rivets ⎪ in plastic			
Needles and thread ⎬ tube			
Darning cotton ⎭	18		
100 Halazone tablets	1½		
Toilet kit	11		
Toilet paper 500 sheets in water-			
proof bag	6		
Flashlight	3		
2 candles	3		
300 waterproofed matches in can	4½		
Fire starter, ½ package	7	3	11
30 rifle cartridges		2	4
Cook kit:			
Frying pan			
Pot and cover			
Coffeepot			
Mixing pan			
2 plates			
2 cups			
2 spoons			
2 forks			
2 knives			
Spatula			
Salt shaker			
Dish towel			
Dishcloth			
6 soap pads			
Grease can			
Bag		5	10
Ax, with sheath		4	0
		23	7

The complete outfit will shape up like this:

	Pounds	Ounces
1 tumpline	1	4
2 bags; bedding and clothing	38	14
1 pack; general equipment	23	7
Grub sack, on pack board	41	12
2 rifles, in sheaths	18	0
For a total of	123	5

and offer the possibility of getting pretty far off the highway, on foot. The load could be split up to give one man:

the tumpline	1	4
the two bed rolls	38	14
and the pack of general equipment	23	7
	63	9

and his partner:

the grub sack	41	12
and the two rifles	18	0
	59	12

This would be heavy toting, but it could be managed for a short trek into desirable country beyond the trail's end. One man could hike out and back with another week's supply of grub, toilet paper, matches, soap, and so on, if the stay were prolonged.

Back-Pack Outfit for Hiking
40 Pounds

Back-Pack Outfit

Back-packers, traveling on foot or bicycle, are offered a whole range of extralight equipment, which provides the essentials of comfort in surprisingly compact form. As an example, the outfit next listed weighs but 40 pounds and yet lacks nothing really needed for a week of one-man cruising. Of course, such a "vest pocket" rig affords but scant conveniences and luxury, but it will take you in and out of the woods and over trails where a heavierladen man would bog down.

	Pounds	Ounces
Frame pack	4	8
Tent, Mountaineer, 4′ × 6½′ × 4′	3	12
Sleeping bag, eider-down filled	3	0
Cook kit, Boy Scout model with some extras:		
Frying pan with folding handle		
Pail with cover		
Deep dish		
Aluminum cup (use for mixing syrup, milk, etc.)		
Fork and spoon		
Spatula blade, to fit on fork		
Enamelware cup		
Dish towel		
Dishcloth		
6 soap pads	2	2
Ax, in leather sheath	1	0
First-aid kit:		
2 sterile gauze pads, 3″ × 3″		
5 yards of 1½″ sterile gauze bandage		
6 finger bandages		
Small tube of Unguentine		
½ ounce boric acid powder		
¼ ounce metaphen or Mercurochrome		3
Toilet kit:		
Comb		
Toothbrush and paste		
Soap and towel		4½
Poncho, neoprene	1	0

	Ounces	Pounds	Ounces
Spare clothing:			
Sweater	8		
Pair of socks	3		11
Repair kit:			
File, 4- or 5-inch	½		
Whetstone	1		
Plastic tube containing:			
Ferrule cement			
1 rod tip			
2 rod guides			
4 buttons			
2 needles			
Button thread, on card	1½		3
150 waterproofed matches, in plastic tube			2½
150 sheets of toilet paper, in waterproof pouch			2
Candle			1½
Bottle of bug repellent			6
100 Halazone tablets			1½
Fly rod			7½

	Ounces		
Fly tackle:			
Single-action reel and enameled line	5		
Filled fly box, aluminum	4		
Filled leader box, aluminum	1½		
Can of Mucilin	1		11½
4 packs of cigarettes or package of tobacco			4
Camera and films		2	0
		21	0
Food for 1 week, as listed under "Backpacker's ration" (page 205)		19	0
		40	0

Such items as the frame pack, Mountaineer tent and eiderdown sleeping bag are quite expensive. You may wish to substitute pack board, pup tent and blankets, at a cost of about 4 additional pounds. The outfit would then shape up as follows:

	Pounds	Ounces
Pack board and pack sack	5	12
Pup tent, 5' × 7' × 3½'	3	8
2 wool blankets, 3 pounds each	6	0
Cook kit	2	2
Ax	1	0
First-aid kit	0	3
Toilet kit	0	4½
Poncho	1	0
Sweater	0	8
Pair of socks	0	3
Repair kit	0	3
Matches	0	2½
Toilet paper	0	2
Candle	0	1½
Bug repellent	0	6
Halazone tablets	0	1½
Fly rod	0	7½
Tackle	0	11½
Smoking	0	4
Camera and film	2	0
Food	19	0
	44	0

There is a most excellent source of information on ultra-lightweight camp equipment which no prospective back-packer should overlook. It is: The Potomac Appalachian Trail Club, 808 Seventeenth Street N.W., Washington, D.C.

P.A.T.C. publishes a booklet entitled *Hiking, Camping, Winter Sports and Trail-Making Equipment* which details a great many items of equipment and names the sources of supply. You could peruse 500 catalogues and get less pertinent information than this modest publication affords for 25 cents. I suggest that you send for a copy.

VI

WHERE TO GO

You should know, very definitely, where you are going and how to get there before packing your duffel and embarking on a camping trip — that is, if you hope to avoid disappointment and wasted effort. Lots of places which "look good on the map" afford little but disillusionment when you get to them, and hearsay is usually a will-o'-the-wisp, at best.

I hate to think of all the "wilderness" riverbanks I have found lined with cottages and the innumerable "no trespass" signs which have barred me from choice forests in country which I assumed to be wild and uninhabited. The worst beating I ever experienced outdoors came from a stretch of river marked "the finest canoe trip in the State" on a tourist bureau map. I doubt that the map maker had run the river in twenty years or more. So I contend that up-to-date personal experience is the only reliable guide to any territory and a professional woodsman is the best source of worthwhile information.

All of our states and the Canadian Provinces maintain conservation departments, whose officers are afield constantly and in intimate contact with local conditions. I am sure you could address any one of them and get in touch with a ranger or warden in the territory you wanted to visit.

Addresses are as follows:

UNITED STATES

ALABAMA:	Department of Conservation, Montgomery.
ALASKA:	Alaska Game Commission, Juneau.
ARIZONA:	State Game Warden, Phoenix.
ARKANSAS:	Game and Fish Commission, Little Rock.
CALIFORNIA:	Division of Fish and Game, San Francisco.
COLORADO:	State Game and Fish Department, Denver.
CONNECTICUT:	Superintendent of Fisheries and Game, Hartford.
DELAWARE:	Chief Game and Fish Warden, Dover.
DISTRICT OF COLUMBIA:	Metropolitan Police, Washington.
FLORIDA:	Commissioner of Game and Fresh Water Fish, Tallahassee.
GEORGIA:	State Game and Fish Commission, Atlanta.
IDAHO:	Department of Fish and Game, Boise.
ILLINOIS:	Department of Conservation, Springfield.
INDIANA:	Division of Fish and Game, Indianapolis.
IOWA:	State Conservation Commission, Des Moines.
KANSAS:	Director, Fish and Game Commission, Pratt.
KENTUCKY:	Director, Game and Fish Division, Frankfort.
LOUISIANA:	Commissioner Conservation, Court Building, New Orleans.
MAINE:	Commissioner of Inland Fisheries and Game, Augusta.
MARYLAND:	State Game Warden, Munsey Building, Baltimore.
MASSACHUSETTS:	Director, Division of Fisheries and Game, 15 Ashburton Place, Boston.
MICHIGAN:	Director, Department of Conservation, Lansing.
MINNESOTA:	Department of Conservation, St. Paul.
MISSISSIPPI:	Director of Conservation, Jackson.
MISSOURI:	Conservation Commission, Jefferson City.
MONTANA:	State Fish and Game Warden, Helena.
NEBRASKA:	Game, Forestation and Parks Commissioner, Lincoln.
NEVADA:	State Fish and Game Commission, Reno.
NEW HAMPSHIRE:	Fish and Game Department, Concord.
NEW JERSEY:	Secretary, Board of Fish and Game Commissioners, Trenton.
NEW MEXICO:	State Game Warden, Santa Fe.
NEW YORK:	Department of Conservation, Albany.
NORTH CAROLINA:	Division of Game and Inland Fisheries, Raleigh.
NORTH DAKOTA:	Game and Fish Commissioner, Bismarck.

OHIO:	Division of Conservation and Natural Resources, Columbus.
OKLAHOMA:	Game and Fish Commission, Oklahoma City.
OREGON:	Game Commission, 616 Oregon Building, Portland.
PENNSYLVANIA:	Game Commissioners, Harrisburg.
RHODE ISLAND:	Division of Fish and Game, State House, Providence.
SOUTH CAROLINA:	Chief Game Warden, Columbia.
SOUTH DAKOTA:	Game and Fish Commission, Pierre.
TENNESSEE:	State Director of Game and Fish, Nashville.
TEXAS:	Game, Fish, and Oyster Commission, Austin.
UTAH:	Fish and Game Commissioner, Salt Lake City.
VERMONT:	Fish and Game Director, Montpelier.
VIRGINIA:	Commissioner Game, Inland Fisheries, Richmond.
WASHINGTON:	Department of Game, Smith Tower, Seattle.
WEST VIRGINIA:	Conservation Commission, Charleston.
WISCONSIN:	Conservation Director, Madison.
WYOMING:	State Game and Fish Commission, Cheyenne.

CANADA

ALBERTA:	Game Commissioner, Edmonton.
BRITISH COLUMBIA:	Game Commissioner, 540 Howe Street, Vancouver.
MANITOBA:	Director of Game and Fisheries, Winnipeg.
NEW BRUNSWICK:	Chief Game Warden, Fredericton.
NORTHWEST TERRITORIES:	Department Fisheries and Lands, Parks and Forests Branch, Department Mines and Resources, Ottawa.
NOVA SCOTIA:	Department of Lands and Forests, Halifax.
ONTARIO:	Department of Game and Fisheries, Toronto.
PRINCE EDWARD ISLAND:	Game Inspector, Provincial Treasury Department, Charlottetown.
QUEBEC:	General Superintendent, Department of Fish and Game, Quebec.
SASKATCHEWAN:	Game Commissioner, Regina.
YUKON:	Controller, Dawson.

OTHERS

| NEWFOUNDLAND: | Secretary, Department of Natural Resources, St. Johns. |
| MEXICO: | Secretaria de Agricultura y Fomento, San Jacinto, Federal District. |

Other fine sources of information are:

Director, National Park Service, Merchandise Mart, Chicago 5, Illinois.

Agricultural Department, U. S. Forest Service, Washington 25, D. C.

Maps may be obtained from these sources by first writing for a list of available issues and subsequently placing an order for those wanted.

Other government agencies issue maps in considerable variety. The Director, Coast and Geodetic Survey, Washington 25, D. C., will send you free illustrated index sheets giving prices of nautical charts and large-scale maps of certain areas along the coasts of the United States.

The Director, Geological Survey, Washington 25, D. C., will send you free a circular giving general information concerning geological survey maps, which include planimetric maps compiled from air photographs; geologic maps covering mineral deposits; base maps of each state and Alaska; topographic maps of numerous areas. The last-mentioned are very fine and well worth having, but every state has not yet been fully covered. Ask for an index circular on the state of your particular interest.

United States Lake Survey Office, 630 Federal Building, Detroit 26, Michigan, issues charts of the Great Lakes and connecting waters, St. Lawrence River, Lake Champlain, Lake-of-the-Woods, and Rainy Lake. A catalogue may be had upon application.

Superintendent of Documents, Government Printing Office, Washington 25, D. C., will send you free, Price List 53 Maps, if you are interested in the complete list of government issues.

In Canada, the Deputy Minister, Department of Lands, in any particular province will give you information on maps issued by his office.

The Surveyor General, Legal Surveys and Map Service, Department of Mines and Resources, Labelle Building, Ottawa, Ontario, issues a price list of general maps and index sheets covering a great range of detailed maps. You should specify the region of your particular interest when applying for one of the index sheets.

Once you are in touch with a ranger or warden qualified to advise you, make your request for information very explicit. Men of that type are not prone to write long-winded letters and you should afford the means of easy response. State just what you want: a good camp site in hunting or fishing territory, a canoe route of specified duration, or a trail for hiking. Mention your experience, or lack of it, to assure a recommendation within your limitations. Ask such questions as:

What is the best jumping-off place?
How may I get there?
Can I get supplies locally?
Can I rent a canoe there?
Will I require a guide?
Will you recommend one?
Is bait available?
What is the best fishing (or hunting) season?
What kind of licenses are required?
Where shall I get them?
Will I need a fire permit?
Where shall I get it?
May I cut tent poles and firewood?
What seasons are worst for:
  Rain
  Ticks
  Mosquitoes
  Flies
Are there any poisonous snakes?
Are there any poisonous plants?

Are the nights very cold?
Is pure drinking water plentiful?
Where can I get a good map of the territory?
What is the compass variation?
Are the natives friendly?

Leave enough space for an answer adjacent to each question, and enclose a self-addressed, stamped envelope for the reply.

If a guide is recommended, get in touch with him and discover if he has a tent and bedding for his own use. Make a definite agreement with him as to wages and time of engagement.

You can make sure of successful and enjoyable expeditions if you follow some such procedure, and I hope you do so when planning to invade strange territory.

Once you have decided on a scene of operations, make sure that your outfit will get there in good condition. Stencil your initials or mark on each package, pack everything for rough handling and see to it, personally, that every item gets in and out of the baggage car. A few cigars, distributed among the baggage men, will be a good investment.

If you travel by automobile, guard against rough edges or sharp corners which might chafe or cut your duffel.

When you transfer, check your equipment carefully, so that nothing will be left behind.

At the jumping-off place, load your stuff in the boat or canoe as if you were preparing to run rapids. It hurts just as much to lose equipment while ferrying a pond as it does to founder in the wildest storm.

Anything tossed carelessly onto a pack animal or a vehicle is liable to damage or loss, regardless of the journey in prospect. Stow it securely, if only for a ten-minute carry.

VII

CANOE TRAVEL

Canoes

Much as I would like to deal with the possibilities of fun afforded by rafts and rowboats, and even express cruisers, my subject is camping, and to a camper the canoe offers more than any other craft. It may be carried just about anywhere, and pushed through narrow and shallow waters impassable to less graceful hulls. It may be propelled with modest effort, without depriving the navigator of any of the sights or sounds in the solitude he has come so far to enjoy. It is rugged and safe as well, requiring a minimum of attention and maintenance.

We have come a long way from the flimsy birch-bark canoes and clumsy dugouts of the aborigines. Modern craft are offered in the light metals, plastics and bonded wood, with advantages claimed for each. I find one principal fault with these innovations: it is most difficult, if not impossible, to repair them on the trail. True, they are tough and strong, but what if you do just happen to poke a hole in one? Can you patch it without the aid of an elaborate repair kit? I'm afraid not.

If your circumstances allow disregard of the repair feature, the ultramodern hulls afford some advantages not to be scorned. They are very light, for one thing. As an example, aluminum canoes may be as much as 30 pounds lighter than canvas-covered craft of similar dimensions. Also, their weight is not subject to increase from waterlogging and successive coats of paint. Ordinarily, they are equipped with air chambers at each end, thus providing a safety factor more dependable than the natural buoyancy of wood construction. Metal canoes have been tested in very tough water and come through without serious damage, so I assume you could take pretty long chances with one, except in remote wilderness.

The plastic and bonded wood models are also light and tough, with a tendency to bounce off snags and rocks rather than crack up in a collision. No doubt you might use one for years and find it entirely satisfactory if utter catastrophe did not overtake you. I have noticed one poor feature of the plastic canoe now on the market — its thwarts are not properly spaced for lifting and carrying. Give that serious consideration if you think of using one in the woods.

The canvas-covered canoe has long been the favorite conveyance of *voyageurs* in the North Woods, where streams and lakes are the principal avenues of travel. It is light and strong, as well as watertight, and will survive a surprising amount of hard usage. For ordinary use, the Guides model, 18 feet long, is just about standard, although much larger canoes are built for heavy freighting and lightweight craft may be had for special purposes. There are also canoes with transom sterns, for use with outboard motors.

The Guides canoe is distinguished by its low bows, which offer the least resistance to wind, and its broad, flat bottom, which affords great carrying capacity with shallow draft. It will safely carry two big men with a heavy outfit and handle smartly in rough water. Its weight averages about 85 pounds.

Smaller canoes, weighing as little as 45 pounds, provide easy portaging for those who travel light, but their capacity is somewhat limited and they are apt to be cranky in heavy weather. A total weight of 600 pounds is about the maximum safe load for such craft.

The science of propelling a canoe is not difficult to learn, but is best taught by experience and I shall not attempt much of a description. Briefly, propulsion and direction are achieved with each stroke of the paddle, the surface of the blade being turned more or less parallel with the keel as the stroke nears completion. In this position the blade serves as a rudder, for an instant. Brief instruction will give you the knack of it. Perfect this trick of steering with your driving stroke and avoid the trailing of the paddle so common with amateurs. This applies mostly to the stern paddler, but the bow man also has something to learn, other than simply pushing back the water. If you work on the problem for a couple of hours under expert supervision you should become quite adept.

A canoe must be "trimmed" to sit nearly level on the water. That means balancing the load so that it is evenly distributed; end to end and side to side. Some advocate a high prow for going upstream and into the wind and a low prow for going downstream and before the wind, but I get pretty good results with both ends nearly level. Every canoe seems to handle just a bit differently than others, however, and a good practice is to feel out your craft and trim accordingly.

Portaging

Before loading your canoe, tie a 20- or 25-foot length of $\frac{3}{16}$-inch Manila rope to the thwarts in each end, or to the mooring rings if there are any. These lines will serve to hold the boat steady when you are out of it, perhaps guiding it through water too rough for navigation. You might also loop a couple of 18-inch thongs on each gunwale,

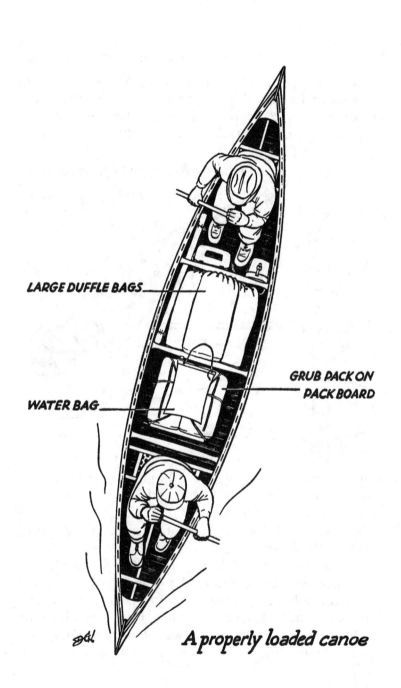

LARGE DUFFLE BAGS

GRUB PACK ON
PACK BOARD

WATER BAG

A properly loaded canoe

about 4 feet apart, with which to tie up fishing rods, safely out from under foot. Four more such thongs, looped on the center and forward thwarts, will serve to fasten the paddles in place as a carrying yoke. This is portage business, in

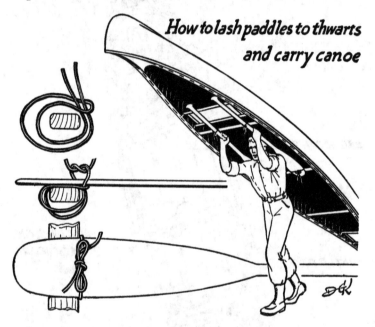

How to lash paddles to thwarts and carry canoe

which the paddle blades are lashed to the center thwart, to rest on the carrier's shoulders, and the shafts project forward to serve as handlebars.

We may as well look into the job of lifting and carrying a canoe, at this point.

Get the canoe into position alongside firm footing. Tip it on its side, with the keel toward you and the bow to your right. Reach down and grasp the center thwart, close to the lower gunwale, with your right hand. Take hold with your left hand, close to the upper gunwale. Push your right knee against the bottom; get set for a heave and toss the canoe

up and over your head. Don't *lift* it — *toss* it! Let down the
canoe with the center thwart across your left shoulder; shift
your right hand to the nearest paddle shaft and turn your
body to face forward, shrugging your shoulders under the

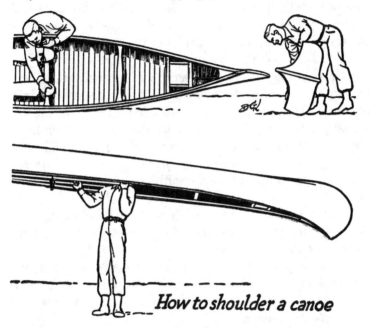

How to shoulder a canoe

paddle blades, forward of the thwart, as you do so. Grasp the
left paddle shaft with your left hand; feel for the balance
and walk into the woods. It's a lot easier than it sounds and
requires much less strength than you imagine.

   To put the canoe down, shrug out from under the paddle
blades, while turning the body so as to get the center thwart
on your left shoulder. Shift your hands to maintain balance
and end up with a right-hand grasp on the thwart back of
your head, and a left-hand grasp on the other end of it. Lift
the canoe over your head, roll it down onto your bent knee
and thence to the ground.

A two-man carry may be accomplished by tipping the canoe on its side with the gunwales toward the men, each of whom then grasps the upper gunwale with one hand and lifts it to his shoulder. Both should be facing in the direction of travel, of course, and be in position at opposite ends of the craft. This is a fairly awkward method of carrying, as the canoe impedes free movement of the carriers' bodies and tends to keep them off balance. Undergrowth adjacent to a narrow trail may afford considerable hindrance, also.

Another method is to turn the canoe bottom up and raise one end high enough for a man to stand under it. He can support it with raised hands under the gunwales, while his partner gets into similar position under the other end. This carrying position becomes very tiring in a short while and presents the danger of a bad spill should one man slip or fall.

A better scheme is to fasten a yoke to the gunwales, amidship, and let one man carry while the other balances the craft or holds up the rear end.

Canoe-carrying yokes are offered by many outfitters and are quite practical when extra bulk and weight are of little importance. They are usually about 38 inches long and weigh 3½ pounds or so.

A pair of heavy socks, or similar padding, may be stuffed into the shoulders of jacket or shirt to afford comfort when using paddles in lieu of a yoke.

Navigation

Navigation of a canoe is largely a matter of caution, so far as the beginner is concerned. In time, you will learn to spot the telltale "V" on the upstream sides of rocks and snags, the riffles over shoals and the whitecaps in rapids. For a start, avoid everything that looks dangerous, and tie up to the bank for a look-see before attempting fast water. When you find it impossible to portage around a bad spot, survey the possibility of easing your craft along the bank by means of your mooring lines; up to your waist in the water, if necessary. Give rocks in the stream the widest berth possible, but don't risk an upset by shoving off one too vigorously. Avoid fetching up broadside-to against any obstruction in a current, as you might tip and fill, in such position. Don't drift into fast water. Keep your canoe under control at all times.

Paddling from a kneeling position will lower the center of gravity when in rough water. If you have to ride out a blow on a big lake, it may be expedient to lie down in the canoe. In any event, stay with your craft; it will support two swimming men, even if filled with water.

Repairs

The canoe is most likely to suffer damage in a broadside collision, with a broken plank as the result. If this should happen, get ashore, unload the boat and let the canoe dry before attempting repairs. You may then replace a shattered section, between ribs, by carefully cutting out the jagged ends and fitting in a piece from the spare in your repair kit. Fasten this to the canvas and adjacent ribs with canoe glue melted in a candle flame and dropped on liberally. Work fast with the melted glue — it solidifies quickly. With the plank section in place, whittle out something similar to a rib section, to fasten over it. This should be long enough to bear on the planks either side of the patch and might be cut from your plywood breadboard. A more provident circumstance would result from having a 12-inch piece of white cedar rib stock lightly fastened under one seat, where it would always be available for emergency use and

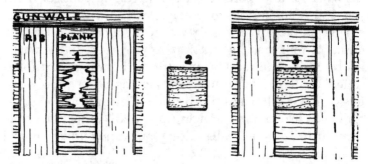

1 CUT OUT JAGGED EDGES VERY CAREFULLY. 2 CUT PIECE OF
REPAIR PLANK TO FIT TIGHTLY INTO PLACE. 3 APPLY.
CANOE GLUE LIBERALLY TO CANVAS AND ADJACENT EDGES
AND FORCE REPAIR PIECE INTO PLACE.

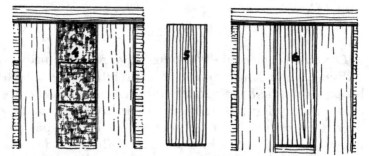

4 APPLY CANOE GLUE LIBERALLY TO SPACE BETWEEN
ADJACENT RIBS. 5 HAVE READY PIECE OF RIB STOCK TO
FIT BETWEEN ADJACENT RIBS AND LONG ENOUGH TO
BEAR ON TWO ADJACENT PLANKS. 6 FORCE REPAIR
PIECE OF RIB STOCK INTO PLACE.

Repairing a broken canoe plank

yet out of the way until needed. Thorough steaming over a pot of boiling water would make it flexible enough to bend quite sharply.

The repair section should fit tightly between adjacent ribs and be glued in place. Screws are not likely to hold in the thin planking.

If the canvas covering is merely punctured, smear a bit of melted glue over the hole. If you have a large rip to contend with, get out your large needle and button thread and sew it together with a "baseball" stitch. Tie a knot in the end of

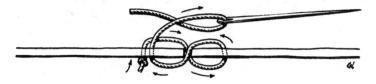

Baseball stitch

your thread and push the needle through from the under side of the canvas, at a starting point about a quarter inch back from the edge of the tear. Pull the thread fairly tight and then start it through the canvas on the opposite edge of the tear, from the under side. Continue this operation until both edges of the tear are brought together, throughout their length. The stitches should be about half an inch apart, if you have enough thread. Otherwise, any spacing will have to do, so long as the gap is completely closed. Smear the seams liberally with melted glue and let it set thoroughly before refloating the canoe.

Don't remove the canvas from any part of a canoe, except as a last resort. Don't tack on a patch — glue it in place. The tacks suggested for your repair kit should be used only on the bows and keel, where frames are heavy enough to hold them.

You may need a setting pole, if your canoe is to be poled against the current. Get a blacksmith to make you a point and carry it with you, for fitting to a pole from the forest. The point should have a socket about 3 inches in diameter, with at least two screw holes in it, and a spike 5 or 6 inches long. Fit it snugly to a straight, stiff pole, perhaps 10 feet long. Don't forget the screws.

A sponge is the handiest thing imaginable for bailing a canoe. It will sop up that last gallon of water which eludes the bailing can. You might tie a sponge of 5 or 6 inches diameter away up in the stern of your canoe, where it would be readily accessible without creating a nuisance in the outfit.

Motors

An outboard motor will afford plenty of ease and convenience, whenever it is feasible to carry one. In the big lake country, many a weary mile of paddling may be saved

outboard motor bracket

by the "kicker" and distances traveled in hours, rather than days.

A one-horse motor will push a loaded canoe about 5 miles per hour in calm water and burn approximately one pint of fuel in the doing. Thus, you could figure on something like 40 miles to a gallon, if conditions were favorable. Ten gallons of gasoline, in two stout containers, will weigh close to 85 pounds; the little motor just mentioned weighs 27 pounds and a bracket to hold it on the canoe will add another 4 pounds. If you can carry that much extra to your point of embarkation, it might be well worth while.

VIII

DOG SLED AND PACK TRAIN TRAVEL

The management of dog teams and pack animals is a business to be undertaken by experts. The beasts used in such service are not pets, in any manner of speaking, and none but experienced men can handle them successfully. Their care and feeding is a profession in itself and the casual camper cannot hope to master it without long training.

I doubt that you will be greatly interested in dog teams, as they are used only when the forest is snow-bound and that is no season for a sportsman to be out for pleasure. However, there may be hardy souls who plan to go in early or come out late and a word of advice may not be amiss. Hire someone to drive the dogs for you and make sure he knows all about it.

Pack trains often afford the only practical means of getting into remote territory with bulky equipment. In the Far West and other mountainous regions, they can negotiate country inaccessible to any other transport. The expense involved is something to consider, of course, but you can make the necessary arrangements with little or no trouble, once you find a contractor. There are many of these, and forest rangers or conservation officers can put you in touch with them.

Your duffel will require careful packing for pack train travel. Canvas bags and the like will not afford sufficient protection from damage if an animal takes a spill or simply decides to roll over a few times. Panniers built of heavy fiberboard or rawhide are required, at least for cooking utensils, fishing tackle and other easily damaged items. In most cases, you'll find pack train operators prepared to furnish such equipment. In fact, they usually provide complete outfits and a camper would be pretty smart to take advantage of such service, rather than use his own stuff.

IX

ABOUT GETTING LOST

Ordinarily, getting lost results in nothing more serious than inconvenience, worry and fatigue. Unless a man goes entirely insane and runs around in circles until exhausted, he can walk out of almost any patch of wilderness and eventually strike a highway or railroad which will lead him to human habitation. There is no fun in such an experience, however, even if there is no danger, and it should be avoided.

Consider a very common example: several hunters park their automobile on a backwoods trail and spread out to work a couple of square miles of game cover. All of them start in a westerly direction, with the intention of keeping in sight of one another and returning to the car in an hour or so. Very shortly, one is attracted by a swale off to the north a bit and wanders away from the general course. Within 15 minutes, he has detoured around several brush patches, gotten behind a hill and lost contact with his companions. The easiest going or the prospect of game influences further deviation and pretty soon he realizes he is lost. So he yells or blows his whistle and the sound carries no further than the nearest rise of ground. He fires the traditional three gunshots and no one responds, because shooting is the order of the day. Finally, in exasperation, he consults his compass, lays a course to the east and strikes out for the starting point. By and by he comes to a trail running more or less north and south, but the car is nowhere in sight. He isn't sure whether he came out to the north or the south of it and decides to go north. After half an hour of travel, with no encouragement, he concludes that he should have gone south and turns around. An hour's fruitless journey in that direction convinces him he is on the wrong trail and he goes east into the woods again, in search of another. Meanwhile, his companions have returned to the car and blown the horn to attract his attention, but he is too far away to hear it. At long last, he finds another trail, but no automobile; accepts the fact he is really lost and wearily plods on to a farmhouse on the wrong side of the township. If his luck is good, someone may drive him to camp for a cold supper and a colder welcome.

Such occurrences may be avoided, easily enough, if the traveler in strange territory will take time to sketch the scene of operations or learn the lay of the land. No one will consider the idea silly if he has ever been lost in so much as a 40-acre laurel patch or tamarack swamp.

Make a practice of carrying compass, pencil and notebook whenever you leave camp, and keep a running record of directions and distances traveled. If you have no map of the country, fix the location of your base in relation to prominent landmarks, road intersections or other easily identified geographical features, and sketch the surrounding territory from a word-of-mouth description. More often than not, such a sketch will require no more time than lacing a boot. Had our hunter, in the example just cited, so prepared himself, he would have prevented the sacrifice of much pleasure, enhanced his reputation as a woodsman and escaped the scorn of his companions.

As he alighted from the car, he would have known that it was parked 6½ miles northwest of a point where the trail intersected a north and south gravel road. He could have asked a few questions of the party's guide and made note of the 80-acre marsh about 2 miles to the west, the creek, a mile north, and the high round hill off to the east a short way. He could have sketched the general direction of the trail, checked his course away from it and taken frequent backsights at the high round hill. He could have stayed within known boundaries and returned to his base with reasonable accuracy, even after considerable wandering, saving everyone a lot of annoyance by being just a little less impatient to begin hunting.

Getting lost in a big wilderness may involve serious consequence. There isn't much real danger of starving, as the human body can function without food for quite a number of days, but thirst, insects or cold might lay a man low in fairly short order. A broken leg could put him down for keeps.

It is a cardinal rule to stay put and let a search party come for you, when lost in vast, uninhabited country, but rarely will an amateur woodsman do that. Pride or panic will often cause him to try and try for a way out, until he becomes exhausted and lost beyond recovery. At best, he may strike out for a known river or railroad and suffer lots of hardship before reaching civilization.

I am no great believer in the traditional theory of following a river out of the woods. True enough, a river gets somewhere, eventually, but its destination might be Hudson Bay or the north shore of Lake Superior. On the way, its banks will afford no highway and frequent detours will be caused by deep creeks and impassable swamps. In lake country, such as the Algoma District of Ontario, a man on foot would be forced to skirt any amount of big water and muskeg, with many a backtrack out of blind pockets, while following a river ten miles. He might float such a course if he had an ax with which to build a raft, but more than likely rapids or log jams would soon stop his progress.

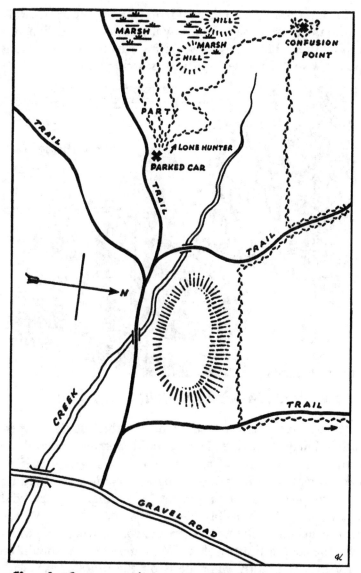

Sketch of projected course and deviation

In dry country a man could reasonably expect to walk out to the nearest road or railway if he knew its location, but it might take him many days, during which his companions would wear themselves thin with searching and worry.

Lost hunter's lopped-tree bivouac with night coming on

Whatever the terrain, the plight of a thoroughly lost person is fairly desperate. During mild weather, mosquitoes could actually finish a healthy man in a few nights if he had no matches with which to light a smudge, or found no mud to plaster on as a protective coating. In very cold weather he might possibly freeze to death.

So it behooves the woodsman to avoid getting lost, whatever the cost in time or effort. Map and compass should be with him constantly when he is off the beaten path, with matches in a waterproof case, a good knife and perhaps a rigged fishing line, as standard pocket equipment — just in case.

Canoe trippers are generally most lax about geography. They assume their course to be concerned only with the waterway, which definitely leads from one known point to another. But what if they lose the canoe, or suffer from some other emergency which requires a forced march to human habitation? Can they find the shortest overland route? Not unless they know what lies beyond the water's edge.

The ordinary pocket compass is not a precision instrument, nor will it infallibly point out true North. It is governed by the Magnetic Pole, which lies far south of the North Pole and somewhat to the west of the 90° West Meridian. This circumstance is responsible for what is generally known as magnetic variation, which amounts to as much as 24 degrees at some places in the United States and changes from year to year. At Portland, Oregon, for example, the North end of a compass needle actually points NNE, and allowance must be made for that, if the location of true North is important.

However, the woodsman usually relies on his modest compass for nothing more than rough direction, and the north it shows him today will be the same north tomorrow, for most practical purposes. In other words, it will point out a straight course of known direction and that is all he needs, in any but precision navigation on a long course.

An accurate watch, running on sun time, will serve the same purpose in morning or afternoon sunlight. Point the hour hand at the sun and South will be indicated by a point halfway between the hour hand and the figure 12. The watch should be held with face up and horizontal, of course.

For casual use, a pocket compass costing no more than $2.00 will serve the camper's purpose. The floating dial model is easiest to use and the fewer figures on it the better. Most dealers carry a good line of small compasses, some of which may be worn in the manner of a wrist watch; others pinned on the clothing or carried loose in a pocket. Any number of American instrument makers market neat models

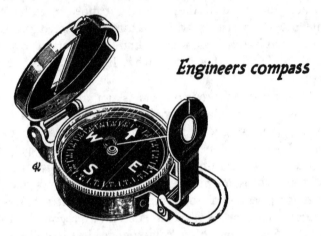

Engineers compass

in hunting cases, which afford good protection and convenience of use. Everything considered, a hunting-case instrument, with floating dial no less than 1¼ inches in diameter and luminous figures, will afford the best all-round service.

There are very fine pocket compasses made for precision work, the U. S. Engineers model being a good example. This instrument has a movable rim, marked in degrees, to provide adjustment for magnetic variation; sights and a practically indestructible case. Sometimes you can buy one secondhand or as Army surplus for $5.00 or less.

Whatever compass you use, give it a fair chance to help you. Gun barrels, axes and other metallic objects are apt to influence it and should be removed from the immediate vicinity. The compass must be used in a level position, so that its card or needle moves freely. Usually, a needle compass has a stop, with which to steady its motion, but inexpensive card compasses more often require slight tilting, to slow or stop the swinging of the dial.

When your compass indicates a course to be followed, take a sight of some prominent object on that course and steer by it. You can't walk along with a compass in your hand and

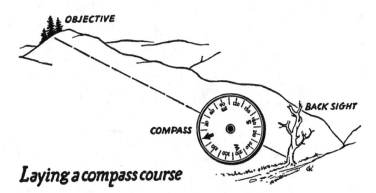

Laying a compass course

expect it to hold steady, as you'll be forever dodging to right or left, avoiding obstacles. Even the motion of a boat in calm water causes the compass card to swing, and navigators often steer by a distant cloud rather than attempt an "average" course.

The compass serves best as adjunct to a map. In the "Where to Go" chapter are listed several sources of maps and there are many others, including your corner gasoline station. Get one to cover the locale of your expedition and carry it with you, working out compass courses from point to point as you move around. A simple method is illustrated, involving no more than the drawing of a line between two points and centering the compass on it, with the north of the compass in exact relation to the north of the map. This done, you may read the direction on the face of the compass — in degrees, if it is so marked.

Often, a published map does not afford all desirable detail and it becomes expedient for the explorer to draw in salient features of interest to him. Copies of maps may be sketched by anyone with pencil and paper, the best mate-

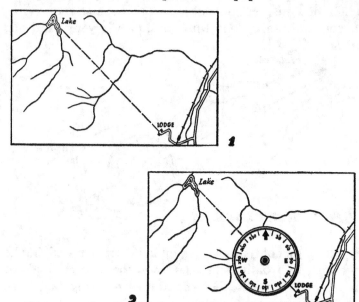

Plotting a compass course on a map

rial being graph paper, on which the squares may serve as a scale. In the illustrated example, the scale is ½ mile per square and distances of travel are shown, including the course of a car from highway to jumping-off place. Direction of roads, streams and railroad is clearly indicated, together with the location of villages and topographical features. Some of these may have been located from memory or hearsay, but obviously the information is sufficient to afford good working knowledge of the locality.

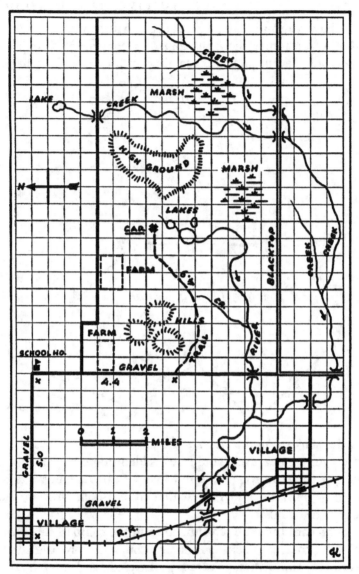

Hunter's sketch of country map with landmarks added

The woodsman entering strange territory without a map should constantly check his course by compass if he expects to avoid the nuisance of becoming lost. The place to begin

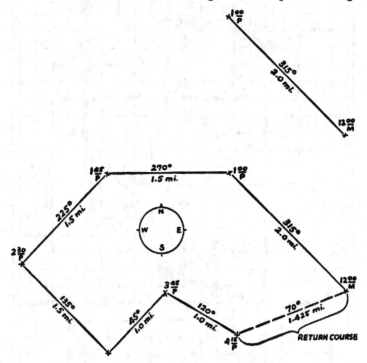

is the starting point and a scale of measurement based on average rate of travel should be decided upon. For example, rate of travel in rough country may be calculated as 1 mile each 30 minutes and represented by a 1-inch line on the sketch to be made.

So, record the time of your start and the compass direction of your course. When you change course, record the time, estimate the distance already traveled and sketch the course up to the point of change. Record your new direction and repeat the sketching procedure at each change of direction. If this is done with reasonable accuracy, a pretty fair estimate of distance and direction to the starting point may be made when you decide to return. The illustration shows directions in degrees, but if the compass is not so marked, points such as NW, W, SW, SE may be substituted, with some sacrifice of accuracy.

X

MAKING CAMP AND LIVING IN IT

Sites

The camp site should be high and dry, as far as condition allow. Gullies, ravines and other depressions are damp and drafty at night and, in some countries, may be the paths of cloudburst runoffs. Sand bars and mud flats not only are apt to be bug-infested during warm weather, but also afford some danger from sudden freshets or floods.

It will be well worth while to spend some time seeking a well-drained, level spot for your tent, where, in summer, the breeze will discourage insects and the morning sun can easily dispel the dew. Keep to windward of marshy spots and other mosquito breeding spots, when you can. Avoid anthills and dense undergrowth which may harbor black flies.

In winter, you'll want shelter from the prevailing wind. Keep out from under big trees, which may fall or shed heavy limbs unexpectedly. They also attract lightning.

Pure water, firewood and poles for the tent are essential to a comfortable camp.

Well-used camp sites are ordinarily stripped of fuel and poles and may be none too private. Also the filth left by former occupants may present a considerable nuisance.

It is good practice to start the search for a camp site about two hours before dusk or suppertime. If you find one

An ideal camp

earlier — grab it; there may be no other within reasonable distance. Every time you postpone this job until the last few minutes of daylight, you face the unpleasant prospect of a hit-or-miss setup, which is bound to cost you comfort and fun. You may also run the risk of a "dry" camp, as safe drinking water cannot be easily located in the dark. The "spring" you hear bubbling from the riverbank may be nothing better than drainage of surface water from adjacent fields and merits thorough investigation.

Drinking Water

Very few inexperienced campers give this matter of drinking water the serious consideration it deserves. Even in sparsely settled regions, streams and lakes are often polluted by farmyard drains and the like, to the end that typhus and dysentery may be flourishing dangers. Running water does not purify itself, as popularly supposed, and local wells afford no guarantee of a clean supply. If you cannot locate a spring issuing from living rock or clean soil, far from possible sources of contamination, boil the available supply and aerate in your water bag. A good practice is to boil water intended for drinking or cooking a full half hour, adding charcoal from the fire in considerable quantity. The boiling will destroy any dangerous bacteria and the charcoal will absorb most of the unpleasant flavors and odors, especially if left in the boiled water overnight. You will strain out the charcoal before use, of course. Add a teaspoonful of table salt to every gallon of boiled water, to give it some flavor.

There is on the market a chemical compound named Halazone, ordinarily retailed in bottles of 100 tablets. One tablet sterilizes one pint of water, according to the manufacturer, and I believe the item well worth inclusion with any outfit to be used in settled country.

Where alkaline water is to be expected, a glass-stoppered bottle of hydrochloric acid should be taken along. One teaspoon of this will neutralize about a gallon of water, so you'll require a minimum of 4 ounces of hydrochloric acid to prepare 2 gallons of water per day for 2 weeks.

Filters do not purify water and are hardly worth consideration.

Making Camp

Firewood is a prime essential unless you carry a gasoline or kerosene stove. Driftwood, rotting logs and pine stumps will not provide good fuel for cooking fires and in some localities you may have to scout carefully for better stuff. Dead branches on standing hardwood trees are generally good fuel, winter or summer. Of course, you may have no alternative but the use of such wood as you can find lying on the ground, as in many regions forestry regulations will not permit cutting of standing timbers for firewood.

When you have located a camp site, each man should proceed with his own set of chores, as previously agreed upon. The bag containing general equipment, such as tent, ax, shovel, and so on, merits first attention. If the cook kit or other impedimenta are in this bag, hang it on a tree or lay it to one side, safely out from under foot. One man should then go to work with the ax, cutting tent poles and stakes, while the other clears a spot for the tent and lays it out.

Any and all chopping should be done with an earnest regard for the dangers involved. Overhead branches or guy ropes can deflect an axhead into a camper's head. Hard knots or stones can afford a similar disservice to foot or limb. Flying chunks or splinters can knock out an eye. Don't leave the ax where it may be stumbled over, or

stick it into a tree so that it can fall on a passer-by. Axes
bite back when mistreated. Put the sheath on yours when
you finish with it, and lay it away carefully.

The knack of erecting a tent is easily mastered when
method is applied to the job. Each type of shelter must

Cutting kindling

HOLD THE STICK FIRMLY ON THE BLOCK AND
SLANT THE CUT AWAY FROM YOUR HAND

Splitting wood

KEEP THE CHOPPING BLOCK
BETWEEN YOU AND
THE CHUNK

be managed in slightly different manner, of course, but the two illustrations will afford a good idea of the general procedure.

For example, consider the 8′ × 8′ Explorer tent. One man can erect this shelter without difficulty by following the steps in order:

1. Clear and level the site.
2. Cut and trim:
    2 shear poles, about 2½ inches by 11 feet
    1 ridgepole, about 1 inch by 4 feet
    5 heavy stakes, about 2 inches by 4 feet
    14 light stakes, about 1 inch by 1½ feet
    (You can measure with the ax handle if you know the length of it.)
3. Spread the tent and stake out the rear corners, AA.
4. Drive two heavy stakes in the positions indicated by BB, allowing at least 2½ feet to project above ground.
5. Tie the corner parrels, CC, to stakes, BB.
6. Tie the ridge, D, and ventilator, E, to ridgepole.
7. Lash shear poles together, 9½ feet from both ends, leaving loose ends on the lashing to tie onto the ridgepole.
8. Lay shear in the position indicated and tie to ridgepole.
9. Stand between shear legs; stoop over and grasp them at FF.
10. Lift shear legs and "walk" them into position. (They will be held upright by the pull of the ropes previously tied from corner parrels to heavy stakes, BB.)
11. Complete staking the tent, including setting of heavy stakes for side parrels GG and poles for door canopy H.

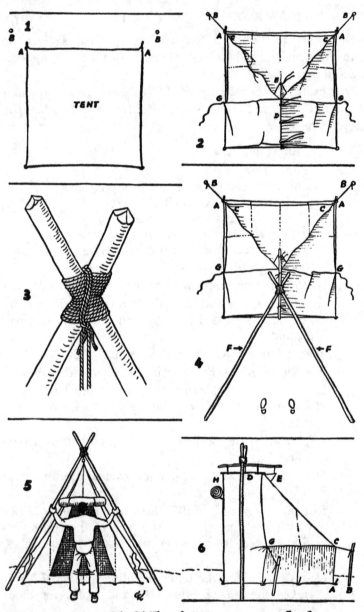

Erecting an 8′x 8′ Explorer tent with shears

Erection of the Explorer tent with "factory-made" poles is even more simple. Stake out all four corners and the corner parrels, fit together the ridge and the center poles, place

Erecting the explorer's tent with telescoping pole

the ridge in position and raise the tent with the center pole. The telescopical construction of the center pole affords adjustment for trim.

An 8′ × 8′ wedge tent may be erected on shears with the materials listed:

4 poles, 2½ inches by 11½ feet
1 pole, 2½ inches by 14 feet
16 stakes, 1 inch by 12 inches

Make two shears of the 11½-foot poles, lashing them 10 feet from the butt ends. Tie the 14-foot pole to the ridge of the tent, allowing 5 feet to project beyond the front end. Stake out all four corners, place one shear under the rear end of ridgepole and raise into nearly erect position. This will result in suspension of the tent from a tripod and disclose the reason for having the ridgepole so much longer than the ridge of the tent. Now, raise the other shear under the front end of the ridgepole, complete staking, adjust the shear legs for trim and you are in business. A canopy may

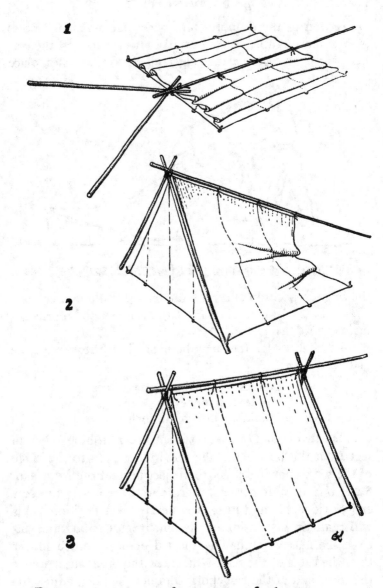

1

2

3

Erecting an 8'x8' wedge tent with shears

be rigged on the projecting end of the ridgepole, or you may hang wet socks on it.

Both men may join in putting up the tent, when preparations are complete. Then, while the ax man is gathering a supply of kindling and firewood, his partner may arrange the cooking facilities, get water, build the fire and start the meal.

Cooking Fires

You will find it well worth while to take some pains with a cooking fire, regardless of convenience or expediency.

Locate your fireplace on a spot of bare ground or flat rock, where there will be room to work and a minimum of dirt and inflammable trash. Gather enough material to start and maintain the fire, including a handful of tinder, plenty of fine and coarse kindling and an armload of firewood.

Birch bark or pine slivers pounded fine are the choice tinder of the North Woods, rain or shine. Shavings from dry wood are good and dead ferns will do in a pinch. Dead leaves will make you wish for the manufactured fire starter suggested in other chapters, or a big piece of newspaper.

Even when the woods are sopping wet, dry kindling may be chopped from a pine stump or split from dead branches under the foliage of standing trees. Dry bark may also be found in sheltered positions at such times. Anyhow, provide yourself with a good double handful of twigs or dry splinters no larger than a pencil, and a somewhat larger quantity of heavier stuff, about as thick as your thumb.

Firewood may be chopped-up branches or split logs and you will need at least an armload of it. Dry hardwood, such as hickory, oak or maple, makes the best bed of coals. Split wood catches fire more readily and burns faster than natural sticks.

TINDER   **SMALL KINDLING**   **LARGE KINDLING**   **FIREWOOD**

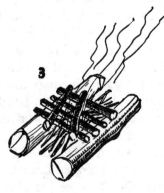

1

WIND →

2

3

4

Building the campfire

To build a proper fire, lay two of the largest sticks of firewood parallel with the direction of the wind, about 4 inches apart. Between these, make a loose heap of tinder, about the size of your fist, and build a small pyramid of the fine kindling over it. Lay half a dozen pieces of the coarser kindling across the parallel sticks and set the tinder afire. Nurse the flame with kindling until it burns briskly and lay on firewood, a few sticks at a time. Don't forget that a fire needs air. If you smother it with fuel you'll put it out.

There will be times, of course, when wind and rain will hinder your fire building. If it is not possible to rig a suitable shelter, with poncho or ground cloth, on such occasions, pitch the tent and build a tiny fire inside, in a frying pan. Once this is burning, you can carry it outside and nurse it into a proper blaze. When tinder is not to be found, lay your little wigwam or pyramid of slivers, twigs or bark and place a lighted candle under it. The constant flame will eventually set fire to such stuff, even if quite wet. Two or three matches in a bundle will sometimes serve the same purpose. Remember that a fire requires air. Pile your tinder and kindling loosely and don't smother the starting blaze with too much fuel.

Once your fire is really burning, with plenty of fuel on hand to keep it going, rig up a pot crane, with two husky forked sticks driven into the ground about 4 feet apart, bearing up a cross member of stiff green wood 2½ or 3 feet above the fire. From this you may suspend your pots on "dingle sticks," chain hangers or what have you.

A dingle stick can be made of a green forked branch, say an inch in diameter, with one side of the fork cut just long enough to hook over the crane and the other of sufficient length to reach within a foot of the fire. Cut two or three deep notches in the long side, a few inches apart, in which to hang the pot bails at various heights. You can lift pots off the fire with a dingle stick.

Now you are all set for boiling or stewing, but there is further preparation to be made for frying and baking. If you can find suitable timber, cut a couple of green logs 3 feet long and 6 inches in diameter. Flatten one side of each and lay them on the windward side of your fire, at a distance

Cooking fire set up

of 3 or 4 feet, parallel with the direction of the wind and about 7 inches apart (flat side up, of course). When your main fire burns down a good supply of coals, transfer some to the space between the logs and you'll be ready to use the frying pan or broiler. If you use a shovel for handling the coals, work fast, so that the implement will not lose its temper by getting too hot. When logs are not available, rocks or mounds of dirt can be built into a fireplace, but don't use wet rocks which may explode under heat. If you have fire irons, lay them across your fire logs and you'll have a setup which beats a grate forty ways.

Baking can be done in a fireplace such as just described. The logs, rocks, or mounds of dirt should be far enough apart, in such case, to allow the baking pan to rest on a bed of stones between them. Heat the stones with a brisk fire for

Baking process

about an hour; brush out the embers and place your cooking, in a covered pan, on the hot stones. Then lay a few slowly burning logs or heavy sticks over the covered pan, across the sides of the fireplace, and a pretty fair oven is in operation. If you keep the cooking vessel from direct contact with burning embers, it will be unharmed, even if made of rather light material, and the baking will come out unscorched. Of course if you find no stones for your oven floor, the bare ground will have to serve and will require longer heating.

I have described but one cooking fire arrangement. There are dozens of others just as good, which you may learn through experience or figure out for yourself.

Don't build fires against, or adjacent to, stumps, trees or fallen timber. You might start a blaze very difficult to control, or leave behind a smoldering spark to touch off a forest fire.

However you build your fire, keep it under control at all times and never leave it unattended for very long periods. When you move camp, put out the fire with water — lots of water — so that no embers will be left to start a forest fire. In sections where the ground is peat or thick mold, a fire will burn a foot or so under the surface, requiring quite a bit of thorough extinguishing. Don't forget that, or you may be the scurvy villain in a forest fire drama.

The cooking will occupy one man's time for quite a spell, during which the other can unpack the bedding, blow up the mattresses and spread the blankets, probably finding time to lay up the canoe, dig a latrine and make everything shipshape for the night, in addition. After the meal, if it is a success, the cook may be expected to bask in his glory while his companion washes dishes. If the meal isn't a success, the cook may go into a sulk, with identical results so far as the clean-up is concerned.

Dishwashing

The onerous chore of dishwashing may be lightened somewhat by a bit of forehandedness.

Rub the outside of the pots lightly with a piece of dampened soap, before hanging them over an open fire. Most of the soot will come off with the soap when hot water is applied, later.

When the frying pan has performed its duty and you have strained off such grease as you want for future operations, half fill the vessel with water and bring it to a boil. Loosen up whatever is stuck to the pan with spatula or knife blade, and toss it out with the boiling water. More often than not the pan will then be ready to put away.

Greasy plates and utensils may be dry-scoured with sand, moss or grass, before washing, as a means of conserving your meager hot water supply.

A dishcloth is short-lived in any man's camp, and wire pads impregnated with soap are a better bet. A half dozen Brillo, Chore Boy or S.O.S. pads will serve for two men's dishwashing for a week and add very little weight to the outfit. The best method of use is to pour a little hot water into a plate, for instance; scrub with the pad and then rinse out with clean water. This is better than holding the plate over the pot and dipping the pad, as it keeps the water supply clean for a longer time.

Dishwater is garbage and will attract bugs. Bury it with your other refuse.

Housekeeping

This business of setting up housekeeping must be a well co-ordinated team play all the way through, with no time out for fishing, bathing or wild life study until the necessary work is all done. Otherwise, someone is going to be the camp goat, with a fine start toward a grudge.

Before settling down for the night, get all of your stuff inside the tent or hung up out of reach of your invisible neighbors, the hungry and curious critters who will be on the prowl before you are asleep. The grub, especially, should be guarded from the minute you get it ashore, as a hungry porcupine will not hesitate to help himself to anything left loose, even while you are watching it. This same porky and his chum, Br'er Rabbit, will eat ax handles, canoe paddles and pack straps, for the sake of the salt your sweat has left on them, so don't neglect to protect them also.

Your fire should be made safe for the night, so that a sudden breeze will not blow embers onto the tent or into the forest. Unless you intend to keep a blaze going, under fairly constant attention, shovel dirt or ashes over the coals before you retire and thus keep on the safe side.

If rain threatens, dig a trench of about 8 inches depth on at least two sides of your tent. This, to prevent flooding of your quarters by accumulating surface water. The trench should not be dug so close to the tent stakes as to weaken their "set."

The morning chores of any camp should be systematized to the point of leaving one man occupied with nothing much more than breakfast, while the other airs the blankets, maintains the fuel supply and cleans up the tent. If you are on the move, packing can generally be accomplished after breakfast by the lucky one who is not washing dishes.

A permanent camp can be made to function quite simply, after the first day. The cook, of course, will devote most of his labor to the commissary and his partner can soon engineer such conveniences as toilet facilities, dining table, stools and clothes racks, which will add greatly to comfort and efficiency. From then on, decent attention to cleanliness and order will be enough to keep the camp homelike.

The washing of socks, handkerchiefs, towels and underwear should be undertaken after the clean-up of dishes, when the use of utensils and hot water will not interfere with the cook's work. Any cook is apt to be temperamental while engrossed with his art, so take no chances.

It is a decent practice to wash and dry the dish towel at least once a day. Custom allows use of a cooking pot for this purpose. Wearing apparel, however, should be laundered in the canvas washbasin, turned inside out. Lukewarm water with lots of soapsuds cleanses woolen stuff without much danger of shrinkage and results will be best if such material

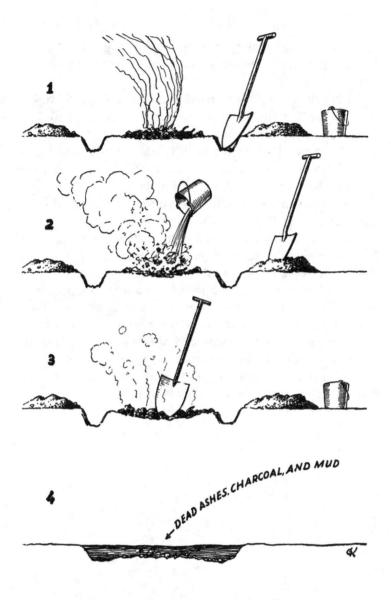

1

2

3

4

DEAD ASHES, CHARCOAL, AND MUD

Fire is out when dead-cold dead

is squeezed after rinsing, rather than wrung. You'll find a half dozen clothespins very handy, if you think to bring them along.

Empty cans should be buried, or burned out and crushed flat, so that flies and mosquitoes cannot breed in them.

Be careful about burning brush which has been cut off your camp site. If there is poison ivy or the like mixed in it, the oil may be carried by the smoke and poison you more severely than contact with the green plant.

Keep a bit of dry kindling in your tent against the wet night and soggy morning which may occur.

Put out your fire, *with lots of water,* when you leave camp! It may be smoldering away below the surface, if the forest floor is anything but hard soil or rock.

You might practice this business of camp-making in some near-by wood lot before starting out to conquer the wilderness. More than likely, the experience would be invaluable as a test of your equipment and skill in using it. Should some little deficiency be thus discovered while you are handy to established facilities, no grief would result and the correction might prevent a lot of annoyance later on.

XI

FIRST AID

If you anticipate calamity, suffer disabilities presenting a constant threat of distress or are so awkward that disaster is forever catching up with you, stay out of the woods until you are better organized, mentally and physically. Otherwise, take it for granted that reasonable care and average luck will enable you to get back home with a whole skin and sound limbs.

Rarely does an informal expedition afford transportation facilities for an elaborate medical kit. And if it were possible to carry provision for every contingency, who would administer it? Unless you are accompanied by a physician, or have professional training yourself, the scope of practical treatment is very limited indeed. On the rare occasions when serious hurt does befall a man in the wilderness, the marvelous stamina of the human body and the ability of companions to carry the victim back to civilization may be depended upon to avert disaster.

Treatments

So, my advice is to prepare for happenstances, taking with you only such items of treatment as you know how to apply. In general, you may figure that something within the following range of possibilities will be all that requires attention. I list them in the probable order of occurrence, together with suggested treatment:

Indigestion

Dissolve one-half teaspoonful of baking soda in cold water and drink the solution.

Constipation

Take a moderate dose of some mild laxative already proved satisfactory for your own use.

Insect Bites

Apply collodion, which you may obtain under the trade name "New Skin," to each bite. Or apply a thick paste of baking soda or a pack of wet salt, or a cud of wet tobacco.

Bee stings should be removed from your pelt and a suction cup from your snake-bite kit will usually do the job quite satisfactorily. Often you can scrape them out with a knife blade.

Once in a great while, a victim of bee sting will break out with swellings similar to hives. Big doses of baking soda, in water, will usually afford relief.

Infestation of seed ticks or chiggers requires over-all treatment with strong salt solution, or water in which tobacco has been boiled, or kerosene.

The wood tick is deserving of special attention, due to her practice of burying her head under your skin. If you pick her off, leaving the head buried, a nasty sore will usually result. Back her out, by holding a spark to her tail. A lighted cigarette or a glowing stick serves this purpose nicely.

Burns and Scalds

If of a minor nature, plunge into cold water. Otherwise, apply Unguentine, Vaseline, a thick paste of baking soda, or a pack of wet tea leaves. Thick soap lather or flour paste will also serve to exclude air, if the skin is unbroken and nothing else offers. Do not pull away cloth stuck to a burn. Cut it loose from the main fabric and soak it with oil or water until it can be easily removed.

Sunburn

Apply Unguentine or Vaseline.

EYE COMPRESS

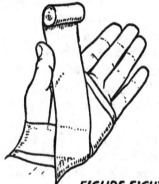

FIGURE EIGHT, FOR HAND & WRIST

SPIRAL REVERSE FOR LIMBS

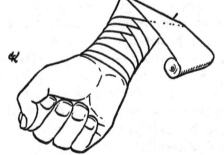

Bandaging

Cuts

Apply 2 per cent tincture of iodine, getting it right down into the wound. Iodine does not heal, being only germicidal in action, so there is no sense in applying it more than once. Let it dry thoroughly before applying dressing.

In dressing a wound, apply a sterile compress and secure with roll bandage or tape. Carry sterile compresses in sealed wrappers, for the purpose. A pad of bandage or other cloth may be sterilized by holding over flame until lightly scorched.

Try not to touch a wound with anything but a sterile dressing. If necessary to wash out foreign matter, use only boiled water, poured on.

In the case of bad cuts, causing excessive bleeding, suspect that an artery may have been severed and apply pressure, with thumb or fingers, on a point between the wound and the heart where you believe the injured artery may pass close to a bone. The body part should be elevated and heavy pressure maintained until a clot forms and the vessel closes itself. You might find it necessary to put your finger right down into the wound in order to reach a point of control, and press very hard for quite a while.

If dark blood continues to spurt, despite such effort, apply a thick, firm pad of sterile dressing, or a roll of sterile gauze, to the wound and bind it on tightly with a bandage. The object of this is to apply pressure to the wound, through the dressing. Do not tighten the bandage by twisting it with a stick in tourniquet fashion. If you do so, or apply a standard tourniquet over a pressure point, the patient will incur great risk of gangrene, which may cost him life or limb.

I know that most first-aid courses favor use of the tourniquet in emergencies, on the assumption that professional treatment will be available within a safe period of time; perhaps 20 or 30 minutes. The wounded man in the woods has no such safeguard, as it may take hours to get him to a doctor. Meanwhile, his companion may let a dread of renewed bleeding overcome judgment and allow the tourniquet to stay in place too long. A healthy person can survive the loss of considerable blood and will be in less jeop-

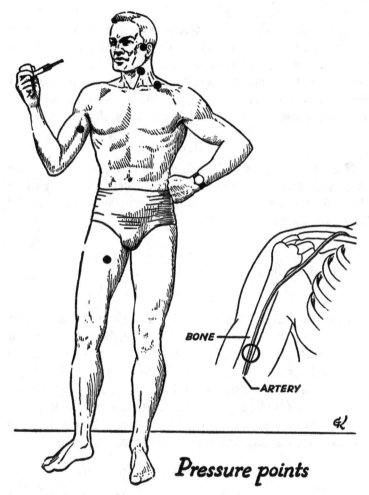

BONE

ARTERY

Pressure points

ardy under the treatment suggested than if a tourniquet is applied in panic.

Do not give any stimulant to a wounded person until bleeding has ceased.

In this connection it is a splendid idea, for anyone who expects to get more than five miles from a doctor, to study the *American Red Cross Text Book on First Aid* and take it with him on his travels. You can get one by sending sixty cents, with your order, to the American Red Cross, Washington, D. C. This little booklet will teach you very explicitly just how to locate pressure points, as well as a number of other aids to the distressed which every camper should know.

Slivers

If the sliver is protruding, catch the end between the edge of a knife blade and your thumb and extract. If buried in the flesh, try a suction cup from your snake-bite kit, or lift out with a sterilized needle.

Chafe

Apply Vaseline.

Blisters

Wash the blistered area with soap and water and open the eruption by inserting a needle, sterilized in flame or boiling water, at the base. Just prick it in one or two places and gently press out the juice. Then place a small, sterile compress over the flattened blister and cover it with adhesive tape. The little Readi bandages are fine for this purpose. If the blister has burst before you could treat it, apply a little Vaseline and bandage as directed.

Bruises

Apply very cold water, or a cloth wrung out in very hot water. Either one is beneficial, strange as it may seem.

Sprains

Before swelling occurs, apply very cold water. (Immerse in running water, for instance.) After swelling, apply cloth wrung out in very hot water until pain subsides and then switch back to very cold water. After some 45 minutes of hot and cold water treatment, tape the joint with adhesive, being careful to avoid wrapping the tape *around* the joint. If an ankle is affected, as is usually the case, stick one end of your tape on the underside of the foot, bring it across the foot

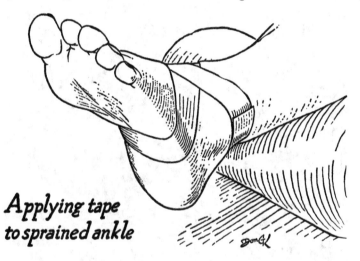

Applying tape to sprained ankle

and part way around the ankle. Alternate the direction of strapping with each succeeding strip of tape, until you have the foot practically suspended, in tape, from the lower leg. This relieves strain on the ligament and may enable you to walk.

Plant Poisoning

Three of our North American plants are poisonous to touch. The most virulent is Poison Sumac, a shrub which flourishes in marshy places throughout the eastern half of the states and adjacent Canada, sometimes attaining a height of 25 feet. Its leaves grow to 14 inches in length, with 7 to 13 pointed green leaflets on each stem, during summer months.

In the fall, they display brilliant red and orange tints, with clusters of tiny white berries among them. The plant is variously known as Poison Elder, Poison Ash and Poison Dogwood.

More widely distributed is Poison Ivy, which trails over fences, rocks and tree trunks in the eastern half of the coun-

Poison ivy

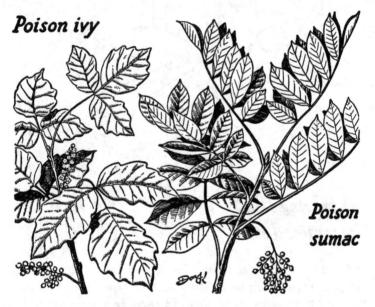

Poison sumac

try, and often appears as a bush. Its leaves bear leaflets in clusters of three, to afford a ready distinguishing feature. The plant bears a small greenish flower in early summer, and clusters of little white berries later in the season. The leaves turn to bright autumn tints before dropping.

A variation of Poison Ivy is Poison Oak, a shrub which grows as high as 9 feet in the Far West. Its leaves also bear leaflets in clusters of three and these are similar in appearance to oak leaves, but smaller. Flowers and fruit are characteristic of the Poison Ivy family.

The symptoms of poisoning caused by these plants are reddening of the skin and itching. Strong soapsuds or alcohol should be applied liberally, to wash off the poisonous oil. Then a heavy paste of boric acid or baking soda should be dabbed on generously, and left on overnight.

Some woodsmen, of Spartan disposition, break the blisters caused by plant poisoning and dab on household ammonia or baking soda. I wouldn't try this on a very large area without cautious experimentation. Take baking soda internally when poisoned; it tends to neutralize the acid of the poison.

Foreign Matter in the Eye

1. Pull the upper lid over the lower, hold it there and blow the nostril on the same side as the affected eye.

2. Rinse out the eye with clear boric acid solution (two teaspoons of boric acid powder in a cup of boiled water) in such manner as to wash toward the nose.

3. Roll the upper lid back over a match stem, so as to expose the eye, and have someone carefully look for the foreign matter, which it may be possible to remove, gently, with the corner of a handkerchief. If the foreign matter cannot be easily removed, place a drop of oil or a tiny bit of Vaseline in the eye, to prevent further irritation, and hike for the nearest doctor. Keep the eye covered until you get there.

I have found a tiny tube of ophthalmic ointment very helpful on two occasions when an eye was injured painfully. Ask your eye specialist for a recommendation on this.

Fishhook Wound

Don't try to back out the hook. The barb will make a nasty and painful wound if you do. Push the barb on through the flesh and cut it off with your wire-cutting pliers. Lacking such a tool, cut out the hook with a razor blade or sharp knife, first dipped in boiling water or sterilized in flame. Treat the resulting wound as a small cut.

Toothache

If caused by sugar, rinse out the mouth with a solution of baking soda. Application of heat, by means of hot sand or hot salt in a bag, or hot water in a canteen, may afford relief. Application of cold is an alternative.

Counterirritants, such as oil of cloves, tincture of iodine and various commercial remedies, are often used but may cause serious complication if an ulcerated tooth or infected gum is involved. Be cautious about applying them.

Earache

If caused by a bug in the ear, shine your flashlight into the organ and he may come out. Otherwise, apply heat as directed under "Toothache."

Snake Bite

Our North American poisonous snakes are the rattlesnake, the copperhead, the cottonmouth water moccasin and the coral snake. The bigger the snake, the more poison he can pump into you, but even the smaller ones of the species mentioned are dangerous. Find pictures of them in your encyclopedia, and study them well for future identification. You will not want to undertake drastic treatment for the bite of some harmless reptile, just because of ignorance.

However, you will immediately suffer intense pain if venom has been injected by snake bite, and further evidence of the reptile's poisonous nature will be afforded by rapid swelling and discoloration of the wound.

Antivenom serum is the only "sure cure" for poisonous snake bite, but it is quite expensive and difficult to preserve in transit, so very few woodsmen even consider carrying it.

The little Compak snake-bite kit is the best thing I know of for ordinary use. It is slightly larger than a 12-gauge shell and weighs just about nothing. To be of any use, whatever, such a kit should be constantly on the person of each man in your party, as effective snake-bite treatment must commence immediately after one is bitten.

The first thing is to sit down. Don't pump the venom all through your system by running for help or chasing the snake. Bare the body part which is injured and apply the little tourniquet in your kit — if you have a kit — between the wound and the heart. The tourniquet does not need to be exceedingly tight. Then unwrap the little cutting blade from your kit, dip it in the little bottle of antiseptic and cut into the fang marks. Cut pretty deep, say one fourth of an inch, and crisscross the wound with three or four cuts about one-fourth inch long. Of course you must avoid cutting sinews, such as those on the top of your foot or back of your hand, so be governed accordingly. The purpose of the cutting is to get a free flow of blood and to let out at least some of the poison. Once the incisions (or cuts) are open, wet the open end of one of the suction cups in your kit (with blood or saliva, if necessary) squeeze the air out of it and apply it to one of the incisions. If the suction cup fails to stick at first attempt, try it again, because you must have suction to get out the poison. Now apply the other suction cup from your kit to another incision, and if there is another kit available, apply the suction cups from it also.

As your wound swells and the swelling spreads, make new incisions, about one-sixteenth inch deep, around the extended base of the swelling and move your suction cups to these.

Don't drink any whisky, regardless of what you have heard to the contrary.

Keep working around the swelling, making new cuts and moving the suction cups quite frequently, so long as the swelling spreads rapidly. In an hour or so, you may work over some of the old cuts rather than make an excessive number of new ones.

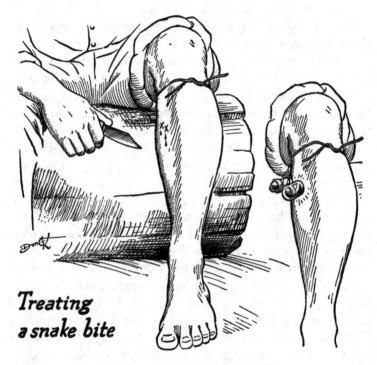

Treating a snake bite

Once every half hour, loosen the tourniquet for an instant, to maintain circulation. If you can't get to a doctor, keep up the procedure, as outlined, for at least 15 hours.

Naturally, if you have no kit the tourniquet must be improvised, with shoelace, handkerchief or belt, and the cutting done with whatever blade is at hand. Sucking with the mouth and squeezing can be substituted for the suction cups of the kit. In all probability, you will recover.

Frostbite

The symptoms of frostbite, or freezing, are white spots on the skin. As these appear, rub them, not too vigorously, with a woolen glove or scarf. Don't rush to thaw out before a fire, as that might encourage gangrene. Stay outdoors or in a cool room; keep up the gentle rubbing with wool for a while and then rub lightly with snow until circulation is restored.

Drowning

Apply artificial respiration and get about it as soon as possible. Keep it up for hours, if necessary. The essentials are:

Lay the victim face downward, without wasting time "getting the water out of him"; prop his head out of the dirt by laying it on one of his forearms; fish his tongue out of his throat, with cloth or sand on your fingers, if he has swallowed it; kneel astraddle of his back; place your palms just about the lower line of his ribs, with thumbs toward his head and fingers on the curve of his torso, and pump slowly up and down. The pumping is done by leaning your weight steadily forward on stiffened arms for three seconds and slowly back for two, repeating the motion over and over. Don't let anyone rub the patient or apply heat, until he is breathing naturally. Don't let anything interrupt you for an instant. Recovery from drowning has been known to occur after hours of artificial respiration, so *don't give up* until *rigor mortis* offers certain evidence of death. When the patient regains consciousness, get his clothes off, wrap him up warmly and put him to bed.

Bullet Wound

Do not wash out, probe for the bullet, or touch with fingers. If a bit of cloth has been driven into the hole and you

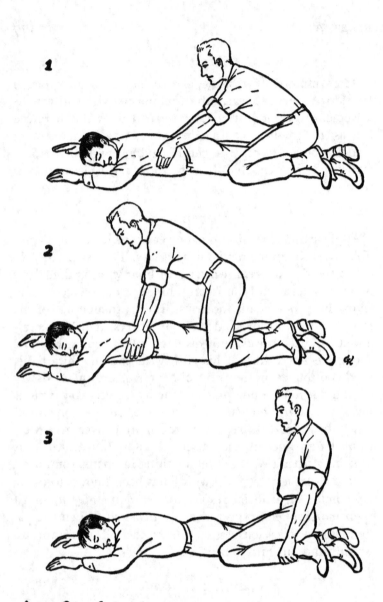

Artificial respiration

can see it, sterilize a pair of tweezers, or a needle, and fish it
out. Dress the wound as you would a cut; apply splints to
prevent motion, if a bone is fractured, and get the victim
to a doctor — quickly!

Broken Bones

Do not attempt to set a fracture, if you have any means of
getting to a doctor. Splint the patient where he lies, moving him not at all until the injured part is immobilized as

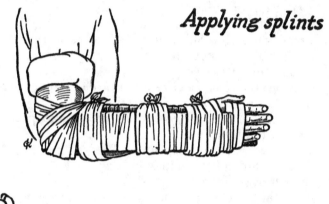

Applying splints

far as possible. Where a limb is involved, apply splints long
enough to immobilize the joints above and below the fracture. Should the spine or pelvis be injured, immobilize the
entire body, with great long splints of split poles or boards.
Pad splints with cloth or bandage, to prevent abrasion, and
fasten them in place with wide bandages which will not cut
off circulation.

First-Aid Kit

A first-aid kit, containing all essentials for the treatments just outlined, can be put together very simply. Gather the items listed hereunder (or such alternates as you prefer) at any drugstore and find a reasonably substantial box to put them in. A little zipper-fastened toilet kit is ideal:

4 ounces sodium bicarbonate (baking soda), in a tin box or screw-top tube
A few cathartic pills in a vial
2 small vials New Skin, with applicators, as retailed
1 small tube Unguentine
1 small tube Vaseline
¼-ounce bottle of 2 per cent tincture of iodine with glass applicator, as ordinarily retailed
1 ounce boric acid powder, in cellophane package or screw-top tube
Two 2½-yard spools of 1-inch adhesive tape
Two 10-yard rolls of 2-inch bandage
12 pads of sterile gauze, 3″ × 3″
Package of Readi bandages, 8 small, 6 medium, 1 large
1 razor blade of the Gem type, with solid back
6 small safety pins
Red Cross Text Book on First Aid
Spare snake-bite kit
Pair of tweezers

You will find that everything will go into a package about 6 inches long, 4 inches wide and 3 inches thick.

XII

FOOD

Food presents no great problem to the camper with ample transportation facilities, as a vast array of easily prepared stuff is available to him. In normal times, nearly everything from olives to Boston brown bread is offered in cans, requiring little more than a few twists of the wrist and a bit of heat to make it palatable. Cooking equipment in any variety may also be taken along, when weight and bulk are of no consequence, to afford the possibility of pretty fancy eating. I'm for that, when it's possible. There's a lot of satisfaction and popularity to be derived from smart operations in the kitchen, and many an otherwise disappointing expedition may be saved from scorn by good groceries. You may garner some worth-while ideas in that direction from the suggestions to follow.

We'll look into the business of feeding two persons from a kitchen during a two weeks' stay in permanent quarters. Assuming that you'll be able to carry in just about anything you want, except ice, I'll work up a menu of good variety but with few perishables.

There will be 15 breakfasts, 16 lunches and 15 dinners; considering the probability of starting out after breakfast Saturday, and breaking camp after lunch, two Sundays later. A couple of meatless days are figured in, for the sake of devout brethren.

The grocery list supplementing this menu is pretty generous. It allows for some accidents and may be stretched to provide a few extra meals for chance visitors. More than likely, you'll have some stuff left over when you complete operations, and it would be smart to make note of the quantities for future reference.

Camp Kitchen Cooking

TWO WEEKS' MENU FOR KITCHEN COOKING (TWO PERSONS)

Breakfast	Luncheon	Dinner
	Head lettuce and dressing	Broiled steak
	Soup	Boiled onions
	Crackers	Mashed potatoes
	Cervelat sandwiches	Bread and butter
	Tea	Canned fruit
		Cookies
		Tea
Canned fruit	Tuna fish salad	Beef stew
Broiled ham	Peas	Corn
Fried eggs	Bread and butter	Bread and butter
Toast and butter	Jam	Pudding
Jam	Tea	Cookies
Coffee		Tea
Juice	Cole slaw	Boiled ham
Poached eggs	Soup	Boiled cabbage
Broiled ham	Crackers	Boiled potatoes
Toast and butter	Veal loaf sandwiches	Bread and butter
Jam	Cocoa	Fruit salad
Coffee		Tea
Juice	Deviled eggs	Corned beef hash
Minced ham omelette	Cervelat on rye bread	Bread and butter
Toast and butter	Pickles	Tomatoes
Jam	Tea	Pudding and cookies
Coffee		Tea
Juice	Asparagus tips	Chicken stew
French toast and honey	Pea soup and frank- furters	Rice
Canadian bacon	Crackers	String beans
Coffee	Jam	Fruit shortcake
	Cocoa	Tea

TWO WEEKS' MENU FOR KITCHEN COOKING (TWO PERSONS)

Breakfast	Luncheon	Dinner
Canned fruit	String bean salad	Frankfurters and
Bacon	Sardines	sauerkraut
Scrambled eggs	Triscuit	Boiled potatoes
Ry Krisp and butter	Dates	Biscuits and butter
Marmalade	Tea	Fruit salad
Coffee		Cookies
		Tea
Juice	Tuna fish salad	Baked beans
Wheat cakes and	Soup	Tomatoes
honey	Crackers	Mashed potatoes
Coffee	Cheese	Biscuits and butter
	Marmalade	Apricots
	Tea	Tea
Apricots	Asparagus tips	Beef stew
Oatmeal	Baked beans	Rice
Bacon	Triscuit	Pudding
Coffee	Marmalade	Cookies
	Tea	Tea
Juice	Corned beef hash	Meat balls
Fried corn meal mush	Crackers	Spaghetti
Syrup	Pickles	Tomatoes
Canadian bacon	Figs	Biscuits and butter
Coffee	Tea	Marmalade
		Tea
Prunes	Clam chowder	Macaroni and cheese
Wheat cakes and	Crackers	Succotash
honey	Cheese	Fruit shortcake
Coffee	Pickles	Tea
	Tea	
Canned fruit	Tomatoes	Corned beef hash
Sausage	Pea soup with sausage	String beans
Wheat cakes and	Triscuit	Biscuits and butter
honey	Tea	Apricots
Coffee		Tea
Juice	Baked beans with	Chicken stew
Wheat cakes and	sausage	Rice
honey	Triscuit	Fruit shortcake
Sausage	Pickles	Tea
Coffee	Cocoa	

TWO WEEKS' MENU FOR KITCHEN COOKING (TWO PERSONS)

Breakfast	Luncheon	Dinner
Canned fruit	Fruit salad	Meat balls
Oatmeal	Soup	Spaghetti
Bacon	Cheese	Tomatoes
Coffee	Triscuit	Ry Krisp and butter
	Tea	Prunes
		Tea
Prunes	Pickles	Frankfurters and
Wheat cakes and	Chili con carne	sauerkraut
syrup	Crackers	Boiled potatoes
Canadian bacon	Raisins	Biscuits and butter
Coffee	Tea	Jam
		Tea
Juice	Pickles	Corned beef hash
Fried corn meal mush	Pea soup with sausage	Succotash
Syrup	Crackers	Biscuits and butter
Sausage	Dates	Apricots
Coffee	Tea	Tea
Apricots	Baked beans	
Wheat cakes and	Biscuits and butter	
syrup	Jam	
Canadian bacon	Tea	
Coffee		

GROCERY LIST FOR TWO WEEKS OF KITCHEN COOKING (TWO PERSONS)

Meat:

    2 steaks, about 12 or 16 ounces each
    Ham, 3 pounds
    Bacon, 2 pounds
    Canadian bacon, 2 pounds
    Cervelat, 1 pound

Canned Meat:

    Breakfast sausages, 6 cans 8-ounce size or 3 cans 15-ounce
        size
    Veal loaf, 1 can (7-ounce)
    Roast beef, 2 cans (12-ounce)
    Meat balls, 2 cans (No. 1)
    Frankfurters, 3 cans or jars (4½-ounce)
    Chicken meat, 2 cans or jars (6¼-ounce)
    Corned beef hash, 4 cans (No. 2)
    Tuna fish, 2 cans (6-ounce)
    Sardines, 1 can (3¾-ounce)

Bread and Cereals:

    Whole-wheat bread, 3 loaves (1-pound)
    Rye bread, 2 loaves (1-pound)
    Triscuit, 5 packages (5½-ounce)
    Pilot crackers, 3 packages (1-pound)
    Ry Krisp, 1 package (7-ounce)
    Oatmeal, 1 package (1¼-pound)
    Yellow corn meal, 1 package (1¼-pound)
    Bisquick, 4 packages (1¼-pound)
    Pancake flour, 2 packages (1¼-pound)
    Macaroni and cheese preparation, 1 package (7½-ounce)
    Spaghetti, 1 pound
    Cookies, 4 packages (1-pound)
    Rice, 1 pound

Vegetables:

    Potatoes, 36 medium, or 12 pounds
    Onions, dried white, 3 pounds
    Lettuce, 1 head (½-pound)
    Cabbage, 1 head (2-pound)
    Celery, 1 large stalk

Canned Vegetables:

    Baked beans, 4 cans (No. 2)
    Chili con carne, 1 can (No. 1)
    Peas, 1 can (No. 1)
    String beans, 3 cans (No. 1)
    Succotash, 2 cans (No. 1)
    Tomatoes, 5 cans (No. 1)
    Sauerkraut, 2 cans (No. 2)
    Pickles, 2 bottles (8-ounce)
    Peanut butter, 1 jar (1-pound)
    Tomato juice, 4 cans (No. 2)
    Corn Niblets, 1 can (No. 1)
    Asparagus, 2 square cans (No. 1)

Fruit:

    Prunes, 1 pound
    Apricots, 2 pounds
    Dates, 2 packages (½-pound)
    Figs, 1 package (½-pound)
    Raisins, 1 package (14-ounce)

Canned Fruit:

    Peaches, 2 cans (No. 1)
    Fruit salad, 3 picnic cans
    Pineapple, 2 flat cans (No. 1)
    Pineapple juice, 3 cans (No. 2)

Sweets:

    Honey, 2 jars (1-pound)
    Jam, 2 cans or jars (1-pound)

Syrup, 2 cans (1-pint)
Marmalade, 1 can or jar (1-pound)
White sugar, 3 pounds
Hard candy, 3 pounds
Pudding, 3 packages (4-ounce)
Baker's chocolate, 2 pounds

Canned Soup:

Clam chowder, 1 can (No. 1)
Vegetable Beef, 2 cans (No. 1)
Pea, 3 cans (No. 1)
Cream of tomato, 2 cans (No. 1)

Dairy Items:

Butter, 4 pounds
Cheese, 6 small foil packages, or 2 foil packages ½ pound
each
Cheese, grated, 1 package (2-ounce)
Klim (powdered milk), 1 can (1-pound)
Evaporated milk, 8 cans (14¾-ounce)
Eggs, 2 dozen

Beverages:

Coffee, 3 pounds
Cocoa, ½ pound
Tea, 60 individual bags or tea balls

Miscellaneous:

Salt, ½ pound
Pepper, 1 shaker package
Vinegar, 1 small bottle
Catsup, 1 bottle
French dressing, 1 bottle
Nut meats, 2 pounds
Lemon extract, 1 bottle (1½-ounce)
Bouillon, 4 jars (2-ounce)
Paprika, 1 shaker package

Celery salt, 1 shaker package
Pimentos, 1 bottle
Toilet paper, 2 rolls
Soap, naphtha, 1 bar
Soap, hand, 2 cakes
Matches, 2 boxes
Soap pads, 2 dozen

Pack Sack Groceries

Obviously, the shifting camp cannot afford a larder so generous as that provided for cabin operations. The weight and bulk of elaborate supplies and the equipment necessary for their preparation would create quite a problem in transport and clutter the outfit to the point of distraction. So the *voyageur* must sacrifice some luxury to mobility and simplify his bill of fare.

Dehydrated foods have been given a great deal of attention during the past few years, largely because of their use by our armed forces. The problem of providing nourishment for vast numbers of men and women located in the far corners of the world has created a demand for concentrated food in nonperishable form which is relatively new to our way of life. Many of us have been amazed by the thought of a full meal coming from a pocket-size package, and yet the idea is not so very new, after all.

Centuries ago, men were setting forth on long journeys into barren country and depending upon compact supplies of parched grain and dried meat for sustenance. Rocka-hominy and pinole were nothing more or less than coarsely ground parched corn and the traditional pemmican of the Far North was a mixture of thoroughly dried venison and melted suet. Corn meal and dried beef are their modern counterparts, adapted to present-day use.

Dried fruits are mentioned in the Bible, as a staple of travelers in the desert, and the humble legumes, pea and bean, enjoy a historical background nearly as great.

So, dehydrated food is not the innovation you might imagine, nor does it completely solve the camper's problem of food supply. True enough, you can sustain life with concentrated rations, but health and enjoyment may be sacrificed in the process.

I recommend the use of only such items of concentrated food as I have found practical in camp cooking. The dehydrated vegetables, excepting potatoes, generally require preparation beyond the means of a camper and they rate no mention for that reason. Dried eggs have a dubious virtue, in my estimation, and I offer no more than the suggestion of experimentation. Powdered milk is more or less in the same category, as I find it none too palatable. Dried fruits, cereals, chipped beef and other such staples of common popularity are given well-merited consideration and I believe you will find them entirely suitable to your outdoor program. At least they will satisfy your hunger while you are experimenting with the novelties. And I hope you do experiment. Improvements in concentrated food are certain to develop and afford many an opportunity to reduce the weight of your grub pack. If you miss a meal once in a while, because an experiment fails, the suffering will not be unbearable.

A word about food for long-range expeditions. It is literally impossible to carry sufficient supplies, by ordinary means, to sustain life for great periods of time. The capacity of canoe, dog sled or pack animal is eventually exhausted, and if replenishment is not accomplished by some other facility, such as an airplane, "living off the country" is the alternative. This is a sketchy business, at best. Game disappears completely at times, and fish then becomes the only likely source of sustenance. That is, in country where fish abounds. I don't know what a man lives on in jungle or desert when game fails him — reptiles, probably. Anyhow, we'll deal with fish for a moment.

Most of us have experienced bad days with hook and line. Smart as we are at finding crawlers under stones and logs, caddis worms in their twiglike cases under shallow water, crickets and grasshoppers in their early morning tor-

por or minnows in a tiny pond where they may be splashed
out, sometimes our finny quarry will not be tempted by
bait. Then we must resort to the net, if we are to eat fish.

A gill net, 4 or 5 feet deep, 30 or 40 feet long and with a
mesh of 2 or 2½ inches will usually catch fish if there are
any. Such a net weighs but a few pounds, without its sinkers
and floats, and should be standard equipment for any party
journeying far into the North. The possibility of licenses
being required should be explored. Stones may be employed
to sink the lower edge of a net and billets of light dry wood
will float the upper. Stake it out in a passage between two
bodies of land, a stream or other promising water. If the
surface is ice-covered, chop a hole every ten feet or so on
the line of your set; fasten the far end of the net to a 12- or
14-foot pole and poke it from one hole to another. Secure
the net at each extremity and harvest your catch, later on,
by retrieving it through a fairly large hole at the shore
end.

Stefansson, the explorer, in his most interesting book,
Hunters of the Great North, writes of living on fish throughout the better part of a winter. The practice was to eat frozen
raw fish in the morning and boiled fish in the afternoon, and
he survived the experience in perfect health.

Enough of that — I assume you are interested in vacation
outings rather than arctic exploration, and want something
more pertinent to your own problems.

Without too much regard for "balance" and other di-
etetic principles, I shall offer a menu for two weeks on the
move, which affords decent variety and palatability, with
a minimum of mixing and fussing. Almost any kind of fire
will suffice for preparation of the meals and many of the
items may be eaten with no preparation at all.

The largess of Nature will not be taken into account. If
you happen to be favored with fish or game or a mess of wild

fruit, you may feast for a while; if your luck is out, you'll be sure of nourishment, anyhow.

The list of supplies is ample to stretch over a couple of extra days, with a little skimping here and there, and it is far from ultra-lightweight. You may pare it considerably after some experience, but for a start it should prove quite satisfactory. The 20 pounds of canned goods may appear excessive, to the experts, but I am assuming that you'll have better luck with your meals if you don't have too many recipes to complicate the cooking. There is also the irrefutable fact that canned food may be salvaged from the bottom of a river and eaten, whilst flour and dried beans are feeding the fishes.

Pounds and ounces are recorded not in accordance with any formula, but to afford a check on alternate items which may have greater appeal to you.

The menus may not suit you, but they will afford some idea of the planning necessary to success. Sloppy carry-overs and excessive puttering are the main things to avoid and you must reckon with a limited array of utensils and facilities. However you plan a menu, match it with a detailed grocery list, so that purchases may be made with intelligence. The list will also serve as a check on future operations, if you keep account of overages and shortages.

TWO WEEKS' MENU FOR TWO CRUISERS

Breakfast

3 days: Bacon, eggs, bread, coffee
6 days: Canadian bacon, oatmeal, cream, coffee
6 days: Bacon, pancakes, butter, syrup, coffee

Lunch

3 days: Salami, bread, jam, tea
4 days: Soup, cheese, pilot crackers, jam, tea
3 days: Soup, deviled ham, triscuit, raisins, tea
3 days: Soup, sardines, triscuit, jam, tea
3 days: Soup, veal loaf, triscuit, raisins, tea

Dinner

3 days: Ham, potatoes, bread, prunes, tea
4 days: Roast beef, potatoes, onions, biscuits, prunes, tea
3 days: Corned beef hash, biscuits, apricots, tea
5 days: Creamed chipped beef, potatoes, biscuits, apricots, tea

Food to supply this menu weighs 77 pounds, including the individual containers. Each item is listed by quantity and gross weight.

The list may be divided into two nearly equal portions, to be packed separately.

Butter is afforded for 6 meals. If you want it three times every day, at least 2 more pounds will be required and add 2 pounds 6 ounces to the total weight.

Evaporated milk for coffee and tea is not included. Four more 14½-ounce cans, weighing 4 pounds 4 ounces, will be required to fill such need.

If you must have real coffee, 2 pounds will supply the 15 breakfasts and add just 2 pounds to the total weight.

GROCERY LIST FOR TWO WEEKS OF CRUISING BY TWO PERSONS

	Number of Meals	Quantity	Container	Gross Weight Pounds	Ounces
Ham	3	6 slices (2¼ pounds)	Waxed paper	2	7
Canadian bacon	6	3 pounds	Bacon bag	3	3
Hard salami	3	1 pound	Waxed paper	1	3
Bacon	9	72 slices (4½ pounds)	Bacon bag	4	11
Dried chipped beef	5	1¼ pounds	2-pound W.P. bag	1	5
Veal loaf	3	3 cans (7-ounce)	Self	1	11
Roast beef	4	4 cans (12-ounce)	Self	3	12
Corned beef hash	3	3 cans (No. 2)	Self	3	6
Deviled ham	3	6 cans (3-ounce)	Self	1	11
Sardines	3	3 cans	Self	1	2
Cheese	4	1¾ pounds in foil	2-pound W.P. bag	1	15
Butter	6	1 pound	Can	1	3
Eggs	3	1 dozen	Carton	1	8
Evaporated milk	11	4 cans (14½-ounce)	Self	4	4
Bread	9	3 loaves (1-pound)	15-pound W.P. bag	5	13
Pilot crackers	4	2 packages (1-pound)	15-pound W.P. bag	4	3
Triscuit	9	9 packages (5-ounce)	2 W.P. bags (5-pound)	6	0
Bisquick	12	4 packages (1¼-pound)	5-pound W.P. bag	3	0
Pancake flour	6	2 packages (1¼-pound)	2 W.P. bags (2-pound)	3	0
Quick Oats	6	2 packages (1¼-pound)	5-pound W.P. bag	3	0
Onions	4	2 pounds		2	2
Dehydrated potatoes	12	6 packages (5-ounce)	3 W.P. bags (5-pound)	2	10

	Number of Meals	Quantity	Container	Gross Weight Pounds	Ounces
Soup	13	13 packages (3-ounce)	{ 5-pound W.P. bag { 2-pound W.P. bag	2	10
Jam	10	2 cans (1-pound)	Self	2	8
White sugar	13	1 pound	2-pound W.P. bag	1	1
Brown sugar	6	1½ pounds	2-pound W.P. bag	1	9
Lemon extract	7	1-ounce bottle	Self	0	3
Apricots	8	3 pounds	5-pound W.P. bag	3	2
Prunes	7	2 pounds	5-pound W.P. bag	2	2
Raisins	6	2 pounds	5-pound W.P. bag	2	2
Coffee — concentrated	15	2 cans (4-ounce)	Self	0	12
Tea	31	62 tea balls	1-pound W.P. bag	0	5
Salt		½ pound	1-pound W.P. bag	0	9
Total weight				77	0

Summary of individual containers:

2 bacon bags
2 waterproof bags (1-pound)
7 waterproof bags (2-pound)
11 waterproof bags (5-pound)
2 waterproof bags (15-pound)
1 aluminum butter can

2 zipper-fastened duffel bags, 12" × 24", 1½ pounds each		3	0
Weight of complete grub pack		80	0

As a matter of convenience, the list just offered may easily be divided into two parcels of nearly equal weight. One will provide for the first seven days' eating, while the other remains undisturbed until required. Such an arrangement saves lots of time in packing and unpacking and helps greatly in dividing the burden, when portaging.

Two 12″ × 24″ duffel bags, with zipper openings on the sides, would be mighty handy as packs, if loaded in accordance with the lists headed "Food Pack Number 1" and "Food Pack Number 2."

FOOD PACK NUMBER 1 — FIRST WEEK

	Quantity	Container	Gross Weight Pounds	Ounces
Ham	6 slices	Waxed paper	2	7
Bacon	1½ pounds	Bacon bag	4	11
Canadian bacon	3 pounds			
Hard salami	1 pound	Waxed paper	1	3
Roast beef	4 cans	Self	3	12
Cheese	1¾ pounds	2-pound W.P. bag	1	15
Eggs	1 dozen	Carton	1	8
Evaporated milk	2 cans	Self	2	2
Bread	3 loaves	15-pound W.P. bag	5	13
Pilot crackers	2 packages			
Bisquick	2 packages	5-pound W.P. bag	3	0
Quick oats	1 package	2-pound W.P. bag	1	8
Onions	2 pounds	5-pound W.P. bag	2	2
Potatoes, dehydrated	2 packages	5-pound W.P. bag	0	14
Soup, dehydrated	2 packages	2-pound W.P. bag	0	7
Jam	2 cans (1-pound)	Self	2	8
White sugar	1 pound	2-pound W.P. bag	1	1
Lemon extract	1-ounce bottle	Self	0	3
Prunes	2 pounds	5-pound W.P. bag	2	2
Coffee, concentrated	2 cans (4-ounce)	Self	0	12
Tea	62 tea balls	1-pound W.P. bag	0	5
Salt	½ pound	1-pound W.P. bag	0	9
Total weight of food and containers			38	14
12″ × 24″ zipper-fastened duffel bag			1	8
			40	6

FOOD PACK NUMBER 2 — SECOND WEEK

	Quantity	Container	Gross Weight Pounds	Ounces
Bacon	3 pounds	Bacon bag	3	3
Dried chipped beef	1¼ pounds	2-pounds W.P. bag	1	5
Veal loaf	3 cans	Self	1	11
Sardines	3 cans	Self	1	2
Corned beef hash	3 cans	Self	3	6
Deviled ham	6 cans	Self	1	11
Butter	1 pound	Can	1	3
Evaporated milk	2 cans	Self	2	2
Triscuit	9 packages	15-pound W.P. bag	5	13
Bisquick	2 packages	5-pound W.P. bag	3	0
Pancake flour	2 packages	5-pound W.P. bag	3	0
Quick oats	1 package	2-pound W.P. bag	1	8
Potatoes, dehydrated	4 packages	2 W.P. bags (5-pound)	1	12
Soup, dehydrated	11 packages	5-pound W.P. bag	2	3
Brown sugar	1½ pounds	2-pound W.P. bag	1	9
Apricots	3 pounds	5-pound W.P. bag	3	2
Raisins	2 pounds	5-pound W.P. bag	2	2
Total weight of food and containers			38	2
12" × 24" zipper-fastened duffel bag			1	8
			39	10

ONE WEEK'S MENU FOR TWO CRUISERS

Breakfast

3 days: Bacon, eggs, bread, coffee
1 day: Corned beef hash, Triscuit, coffee
3 days: Bacon, pancakes, butter, syrup, coffee

Lunch

3 days: Salami, bread, jam, tea
3 days: Soup, cheese, Triscuit, jam, tea
2 days: Soup, veal loaf, Triscuit, raisins, tea

Dinner

2 days: Ham, potatoes, bread, butter, prunes, tea
1 day: Roast beef, potatoes, boiled onions, bread, prunes, tea
3 days: Creamed chipped beef, potatoes, Triscuit, apricots, tea
1 day: Corned beef hash, boiled onions, Triscuit, apricots, tea

Food to supply this menu weighs 36 pounds 15 ounces, including the individual containers.

Each item is listed by quantity and gross weight, for convenience in ordering.

The list may be divided into two nearly equal portions to be packed separately. Thus, one half of the larder remains undisturbed until the other half is consumed.

You'll note that butter is figured in for 3 breakfasts and 2 dinners only. If you want another pound for the balance of the week, add 1 pound 3 ounces to the total weight.

One can of evaporated milk is allocated to the creaming of chipped beef for 3 dinners. If you require cream, for tea and coffee, add 2 more 14½-ounce cans weighing, together, 2 pounds 2 ounces.

A pound of real coffee will be required to replace the concentrated article. The substitution will add 1 pound to the total weight.

GROCERY LIST FOR ONE WEEK OF CRUISING BY TWO PERSONS

	Number of Meals	Quantity	Container	Gross Weight Pounds	Ounces
Ham	2	4 slices, 1½ pounds	Waxed paper	1	12
Bacon	6	48 slices, 3 pounds	Bacon bag	3	3
Corned beef hash	2	2 cans (No. 2)	Self	2	4
Chipped beef	3	1 pound	2-pound W.P. bag	1	1
Hard salami	3	1 pound	Waxed paper	1	3
Roast beef	1	1 can (12-ounce)	Self	0	15
Veal loaf	2	2 cans (7-ounce)	Self	1	2
Eggs	3	1 dozen	Carton	1	8
Cheese	3	1½ pounds, in foil	2-pound W.P. bag	1	10
Evaporated milk	3	1 can (14½-ounce)	Self	1	1
Potatoes, dehydrated	6	3 packages (5-ounce)	5-pound W.P. bag	1	4
Onions	2	1 pound	5-pound W.P. bag	1	2
Soup, dehydrated	5	5 packages (3-ounce)	5-pound W.P. bag	1	1
Bread	9	3 loaves (1-pound)	15-pound W.P. bag	3	4
Triscuit	10	10 packages (5-ounce)	15-pound W.P. bag	4	10
Pancake flour	3	1 package (1¼-pound)	5-pound W.P. bag	1	8
Brown sugar	3	1 pound	2-pound W.P. bag	1	1
Jam	6	1-pound can	Self	1	4
Apricots	4	1 pound	5-pound W.P. bag	1	2
Prunes	3	1 pound	5-pound W.P. bag	1	2
Raisins	2	1 pound	2-pound W.P. bag	1	1
Butter	5	1 pound	Aluminum can	1	3

	Number of Meals	Quantity	Container	Gross Weight Pounds	Ounces
Coffee, concentrated	7	1 can (4-ounce)	Self	0	6
Tea	15	30 tea balls	1-pound W.P. bag	0	4
Lemon extract	3	½-ounce bottle	Self	0	2
Salt		¼ pound	1-pound W.P. bag	0	5
White sugar		½ pound	1-pound W.P. bag	0	9
Total weight				36	15

Summary of individual containers:

3 waterproof bags (1-pound)
4 waterproof bags (2-pound)
6 waterproof bags (5-pound)
2 waterproof bags (15-pound)
1 neoprene bacon bag
1 aluminum butter can

			Pounds	Ounces
Flour sack, for half of supply			0	9
12″ × 36″ duffel bag, for entire pack			1	8
Weight of complete grub pack			39	0

FOOD PACK NUMBER 1 — FIRST HALF OF WEEK

	Quantity	Container	Gross Weight Pounds	Ounces
Bacon	3 pounds	Bacon bag	3	3
Ham	4 slices	Waxed paper	1	12
Hard salami	1 pound	Waxed paper	1	3
Roast beef	1 can	Self	0	15
Bread	3 loaves	15-pound W.P. bag	3	4
Butter	1 pound	Can	1	3
Eggs	1 dozen	Carton	1	8
Potatoes, dehydrated	3 packages	5-pound W.P. bag	1	4
Onions	1 pound	5-pound W.P. bag	1	2
Prunes	1 pound	5-pound W.P. bag	1	2
Lemon extract	½-ounce bottle	Self	0	2
White sugar	½ pound	1-pound W.P. bag	0	9
Jam	1 pound	Can	1	4
Coffee, concentrated	4-ounce can	Self	0	6
Tea	30 tea balls	1-pound W.P. bag	0	4
Salt	¼ pound	1-pound W.P. bag	0	5
Total weight of food and containers			19	6

FOOD PACK NUMBER 2 — SECOND HALF OF WEEK

		Gross Weight	
	Quantity	Container	Pounds	Ounces
Veal loaf	2 cans	Self	1	2
Corned beef hash	2 cans	Self	2	4
Dried chipped beef	1 pound	2-pound W.P. bag	1	1
Soup, dehydrated	5 packages	5-pound W.P. bag	1	1
Evaporated milk	1 can	Self	1	1
Cheese	1½ pounds	2-pound W.P. bag	1	10
Triscuit	10 packages	15-pound W.P. bag	4	10
Pancake flour	1 package	5-pound W.P. bag	1	8
Brown sugar	1 pound	2-pound W.P. bag	1	1
Raisins	1 pound	2-pound W.P. bag	1	1
Apricots	1 pound	5-pound W.P. bag	1	2
			17	9
Flour sack for above			0	9
Total weight of food and containers			18	2

Food for Hikers

I once had a hiker's grub list guaranteed to keep him alive for a week, or long enough to reach a restaurant, and it totaled up to about 14 pounds. The thing afforded pretty drab possibilities, however, so I worked in several meals of ham and eggs, on the theory that he might quit and go home when he got down to the chipped beef and dehydrated potato fare. You may have the revised version, for what it's worth to you.

BACK–PACKER'S RATION FOR ONE WEEK

Breakfast
3 days: Bacon, eggs, bread, butter, coffee
4 days: Bacon, cakes, butter, syrup, coffee

Lunch
3 days: Soup, cheese, bread, raisins, tea
5 days: Soup, cheese, Ry Krisp, raisins, tea

Supper
3 days: Ham, eggs, bread, butter, apricots, tea
5 days: Chipped beef, potatoes, Ry Krisp, butter, apricots, tea

GROCERY LIST FOR A BACK-PACKER'S RATION

	Number of Meals	Quantity	Container	Gross Weight Pounds	Ounces
Bacon	7	28 slices (1¾ pounds)	Bacon bag	1	15
Boiled ham	3	6 slices (1 pound)	Waxed paper	1	3
Dried chipped beef	5	10 ounces	1-pound W.P. bag	0	11
Eggs	6	1 dozen	Carton	1	8
Cheese	8	¾ pound, in foil	2-pound W.P. bag	0	14
Butter	15	1 pound	Can	1	3
Evaporated milk	5	3 cans (6-ounce)	Self	1	5
Bread	9	2 loaves	10-pound W.P. bag	2	3
Ry Krisp	10	3 packages (7-ounce)	10-pound W.P. bag	1	14
Pancake flour	4	1 package (1¼-pound)	2-pound W.P. bag	1	7
Potatoes, dehydrated	5	1 package (5-ounce)	2-pound W.P. bag	0	7
Soup, dehydrated	8	4 packages (3-ounce)	2-pound W.P. bag	0	13
Apricots	8	1 pound	2-pound W.P. bag	1	1
Raisins	8	1 pound	2-pound W.P. bag	1	1
Coffee, concentrated	7	2 ounces	Can	0	4
Tea	16	16 tea balls	1-pound W.P. bag	0	2
Salt		2 ounces	Shaker	0	3
Brown sugar	4	½ pound	1-pound W.P. bag	0	9
White sugar	4	¼ pound	1-pound W.P. bag	0	5
Total weight of food and containers				19	0

Campfire Recipes

Meat

BACON is a staple for outdoor breakfasts and serves also to bolster soups and flavor beans. It keeps best in the flitch (or chunk), but is awkward to slice, away from tables and such. You'll have no trouble with a two weeks' supply if you choose firm meat with generous streaks of lean and have it sliced without the rind. Sixteen slices to the pound will be about right. Packaged slices, put up in cellophane, are convenient and long-lasting, as a general rule.

You may find it handy to cut bacon slices in half, when using a small skillet.

The successful frying of bacon is largely a matter of keeping it from burning, or overcooking. Start with a single layer of strips in a clean, cold pan and fry them slowly over a steady fire. Turn the strips frequently and when they begin to crinkle a bit at the edges, take them out. Place them on a clean cloth or paper towel to absorb most of the free grease, if you can. The strips will be crisper than you think possible, after cooling a bit. If you fry bacon until it becomes crisp in the pan, it will be partly burned or too brittle for good eating, when it cools. You may start your second batch in the hot pan of grease and get good results by turning often and watching closely. Be careful to prevent the grease from catching fire and avoid the explosion which will result from water dropped into it.

Now if you are lucky enough to have a heavy skillet, which will heat slowly and evenly, you can fry quite a quantity of bacon with very little fuss and bother. Stack the slices on edge, perhaps just as they come out of the wrapper, in the cold skillet and cook slowly. The grease will fry out long before there is any danger of burning and the meat will cook in it as neatly as you please. You may want to turn the batch once or twice, but more than likely it will be unnecessary.

This is a good trick to have up your sleeve if you ever need to make breakfast for a large party. In such event, you could stack the bacon in a baking pan and cook it in a moderately hot oven. Four slices per man would be a pretty liberal ration for any but lumberjacks.

CANADIAN BACON is lean, cured pork, similar to ham. It provides no shortening or grease for subsequent use, but is very tasty, broiled in a pan or over glowing coals.

PEA MEAL BACK is a similar article with a flavor all its own — and a dandy! The only place I have found it is Sault Ste. Marie, but there must be other sources in the Dominion. Either of these keep well in reasonably cool weather and will carry through a two weeks' trip, if left in the chunk.

HAM is a fine meat item for the first few days in camp, but it soon molds, unless heavily salted or smoked. You can smoke it a bit extra over the campfire if you get suspicious of it or wish to prolong its usefulness. Boiled ham is a good bet for campers, as it is ready to eat when hot. Slices about ¼-inch thick fry nicely for breakfast and thicker pieces cook up well with beans or cabbage. Leftovers may be minced and worked into omelettes or Spanish rice.

Cured ham is best when tenderized and you will do well to stress that feature when making your purchase. It is handy to carry ham in slices, which, if generously wrapped in waxed paper, will keep fresh about as long as a small chunk.

CHOPPED STEAK should be just that, rather than the "hamburger" concoction offered by some butchers.

For two men, 1½ pounds of good round steak, freshly ground, should be about right. Some like a portion of fresh pork substituted for part of the beef, but that's a matter of individual taste.

When you prepare to cook chopped steak (which should be the first night out, unless refrigeration is available) mix 1½ cups of corn flakes, wheaties, or the like, and ¾ cup of milk with the meat. Work it into patties of the size desired and cook in a lightly greased frying pan or skillet. Fry the patties on one side for five minutes or so, turn, season to taste and fry until done to your liking.

Of course, if no breakfast food or milk is on hand, the meat alone will afford tasty eating when cooked in cakes, patties or balls — thick or thin.

BEEFSTEAK affords the finest kind of first-night dinner in camp. For best results, take along 12- or 14-ounce tenderloins or sirloins, about an inch thick. Without washing, beating or flouring, put them in a skillet hot enough to "bounce back" a drop of water and greased very lightly, if at all. Sear one side of the meat quickly and turn. Season with salt and pepper and cook until done to your liking, turning frequently and pouring off excess fat as it accumulates. You may cut into the steaks with a sharp knife, as they are broiling, to discover the degree of "doneness."

BEEF STEW is one of the traditional stand-bys for outdoor eating and a mighty good one. There are several brands of canned stew on the market, but they leave something to be desired and you can make a better article with little trouble. The basic ingredients are meat, potatoes and onions; with celery, tomatoes, carrots, peas, cabbage and turnips ranking high as supplementary ingredients. Assuming that you'll be working on a simple grub list, I'll offer a packsack recipe which requires nothing more than:

> 3 medium-sized potatoes
> 3 medium-sized dried onions
> 1 can of roast beef (12-ounce)

Peel the potatoes, cut them into one-inch cubes and wash in cold water. Put them on the fire with enough water to cover and bring to a boil. Stir in a scant teaspoon of salt. Peel the onions, quarter them and put them in the pot with the potatoes. (Onions require less cooking than potatoes.)

When the pot has boiled for about 25 minutes, put in the canned beef broken into small pieces. It will be hot enough for good eating, when the potatoes are cooked. About 30 minutes of boiling should be sufficient for the vegetables, but test the potatoes with a fork, to make sure they are soft and thoroughly done. This stew may be thickened with a couple of tablespoons of floor, made into a thick paste and stirred into the pot just before taking it off the fire. A portion each of tomato soup flakes and dehydrated celery soup would improve it greatly, if you had such items to put in about the same time as the meat. Dehydrated vegetables, properly soaked, may be substituted for the potatoes and onions in this recipe, at the sacrifice of some flavor. If you use dehydrated ingredients, observe the manufacturer's instructions; some require more soaking and cooking than others.

CHICKEN STEW may be prepared from canned chicken meat in the same manner as beef stew.

CORNED BEEF HASH is a favorite with most campers and a cinch for the cook. Bring half a cup of water to a boil in the frying pan; dump in a No. 2 can of hash and break it up with fork or spatula. Turn it frequently and add more water if it shows signs of scorching. It will be ready to eat when it's hot.

CORNED BEEF out of the can may be used in stew or hash, but it suits most people better when sliced and eaten cold. A 12-ounce can will provide an ample meal for two hungry men, if supplemented with bread or crackers.

VEAL LOAF is another canned meat item which is tasty when cold. It is packed in 12-ounce and 7-ounce cans, the latter being ample for two portions.

CANNED PORK PRODUCTS, such as PREM, MOR, SPAM and TREET, are somewhat more versatile than corned beef or veal loaf, as they may be broiled or fried, with good results. The 12-ounce cans will provide a couple of slices each for two campers' breakfast, and sandwiches for lunch to boot.

CERVELAT and SALAMI afford sandwich filling for those who like them, but respond poorly to any kind of cooking. Hard salami keeps well in the woods if left in the original form and sliced as required.

BREAKFAST SAUSAGES, in cans, are really something, when served with eggs or pancakes. Sometimes you can find 8-ounce cans, just right for one two-man meal, but more often than not a larger package, containing 15 ounces, is the only one obtainable. You can fry all of the contents, however, eating half for breakfast and making the balance into luncheon sandwiches.

TUNA FISH makes tasty sandwiches or salad and is worth taking along. A small, flat can of 6 ounces provides well for a twosome lunch.

DRIED CHIPPED BEEF comes pretty close to being the most concentrated food available to present-day campers. It may be eaten as is, if you have enough water to quench the resulting thirst, but is best when freshened and creamed. Start out with a cup of milk — either diluted evaporated milk or a solution of powdered milk; ¼ pound of chipped beef; a lump of butter the size of an egg and a bit of flour. Shred the beef, put it in a pan, pour boiling water over it and let stand for a couple of minutes. Melt the butter in another pan, drain the beef and add it to the butter. Cook for three minutes or so, stirring constantly, and pour on half a cup of milk. Thicken the remaining milk with one or two teaspoons of flour and stir that into the beef. Cook a couple of minutes longer and serve on hot toast or baked potatoes. Bacon fat may be substituted for the butter and a tablespoon of prepared mustard, stirred into the frizzling beef, might add a delightful touch.

MEAT BALLS come in small cans and may be served with macaroni, spaghetti or beans, to good advantage. They require no more preparation than heating.

FRANKFURTERS are put up in glass and tin, to afford fine eating with sauerkraut, beans or pea soup. You have long since discovered that they make good sandwich fills also. I cook 'em whole, with sauerkraut, but prefer small pieces with beans or soup. The 4½-ounce package is enough for one meal, ordinarily.

GRAVY is usually little more than meat juice or grease, thickened with flour. There are prepared gravy compounds, however, and several meat-extract products which may be used successfully. You could start from scratch and make good gravy by melting 2 tablespoons of bacon grease or butter, mixing in a handful of flour, adding a cup of boiling water and seasoning with a tablespoon or so of beef extract and a pinch of salt.

CANNED SALMON may be eaten as is; mixed into a salad, with chopped celery and mayonnaise dressing; or cooked, in the form of croquettes or loaf.

The contents of a small can, mashed with a fork, mixed with two eggs and thickened with crackers or dried bread crumbs, will make enough croquettes or loaf for two persons. The addition of chopped onions and celery will greatly improve the flavor. As loaf, it may be baked in a pan for about 20 minutes. Croquettes of the mixture may be fried

in deep grease until well crusted or patted into ½-inch cakes
and fried in a hot, well-greased skillet. Mashed potatoes may
be substituted for crumbs, in mixing.

WHITE SAUCE goes well with cooked salmon. Melt a
tablespoon of butter in a small pan, and mix into it 2 tablespoons of flour. Cook and stir for 10 minutes or so, until a
smooth paste results. Then add a cup of milk, a little at a
time, stirring constantly to keep the batch free of lumps.
Keep the pan warm while adding the milk. Season with
salt and pepper.

Soup

SOUP appears on my menus as a luncheon item, most
frequently, but it is also a dandy fill-in for dinners, when the
larder is low or the appetites especially ravenous. I'll con-
cede that homemade soup beats any other, hands down, but
it often is beyond the skill or facilities of the camp cook.
So look over the canned offerings and the dehydrated vari-
eties in cellophane packages. The latter are just about ideal
for back-packers, as a 3-ounce packet ordinarily makes up
into 5 or 6 cups of good soup; almost enough in itself to
feed two hungry men. Preparation involves nothing much
more than the addition of salt and fat, in the form of butter, bacon grease or meat scraps. Follow the directions on
the wrapper and you'll be pleased with the result, more
than likely.

Here's a mess of pottage that will serve as a full meal,
sometime when you have fish at hand.

Fish Chowder

Clean and skin a 2-pound fish, boil in salted water to cover,
until tender. Drain, saving liquid — separate fish from
bones.

PREPARE:
 ¼ cup diced bacon
 ⅓ cup sliced onions
 2 cups diced raw potatoes
HAVE READY:
 2 teaspoons salt
 ⅛ teaspoon pepper
 ½ teaspoon celery salt
 1½ cups water (use liquid from fish and add water if
 necessary)
 1 quart milk

Fry bacon slowly until crisp — remove from grease and set aside. In the grease brown the onion slightly — then add the water, potatoes and seasoning. Cook until potatoes are tender. Add crisped bacon, fish and milk — bring to boiling point and serve.

Instead of boiled fish, canned shrimp, crabmeat or tuna fish can be used.

Cheese

CHEESE is best carried in the foil-wrapped packages to be found in nearly all city grocery stores. The ordinary chunk of "store" cheese will soon dry out, or mold, in the woods. Grated cheese, for use with macaroni or spaghetti, is put up in packages of 2 ounces, or more. Cheddar, or American, cheese may be purchased in ½-pound foil-wrapped packages and the fancier brands, such as Bleu, Camembert, and so on, are often offered in 3-ounce individual servings.

Eggs

FRESH EGGS are a delightful addition to any camp menu and their transport offers no insurmountable problem. Put them in the individually partitioned pulp-board boxes used by shippers; avoid rough handling and they will usually come through undamaged. The containers mentioned are made of fairly heavy stock, about 1/8 inch thick, and have cuplike pockets in bottom and top for each egg. You may buy them at poultry supply houses and department stores very reasonably. For safety on tough portages, I sometimes wrap each box of one dozen eggs in a couple of sheets of crumpled newspaper and then take care not to drop the pack or step on it.

Grocery store eggs are somewhat of a gamble, at best, and if you find no better source, figure that three days of warm weather will be the limit of their endurance. Strictly fresh eggs will sometimes remain wholesome for two weeks in cool weather.

If you outfit in a large center of population you may be able to find Pasteurized eggs for your grub sack. These will stay fresh, in moderate temperatures, over quite a period of time.

DEHYDRATED EGGS may be all right to mix with pancake batter, or the like, but I find them unsatisfactory otherwise. You can make an omelette of them but it's a rubbery, unsavory thing as compared to the real article. Try them once, anyhow. If you happen to like them, one of your supply problems will be licked.

TO FRY EGGS, break them into a plate or cup and slide them gently into a well-greased, medium-hot pan. If you fry one at a time you may find it possible to turn them without breaking the yolk.

POACHED EGGS are managed about the same as fried eggs, with the frying pan half full of boiling water, instead of being greased. As the eggs cook, splash some of the boiling water over them with spoon or spatula to poach them on top. None but fresh eggs will poach successfully. A tablespoon of vinegar added to each quart of water will serve to set the whites of the eggs.

SCRAMBLED EGGS are usually a second thought with me. If a yolk is runny, or breaks when put into the pan, I whip it up with a fork, as it fries, and smugly announce that we're having 'em scrambled, for a change. You could mix 4 eggs with 2 tablespoons of butter and ½ cup of milk before frying and do a better job.

BOILED EGGS are produced by placing the hen fruit (in the shell, of course) in cold water, and bringing to a boil. If you like them soft, take them out when the water gets to a good boil. For hard-boiled eggs, to carry over for lunch, a simmering of 10 minutes or so, after the initial boil, will do the trick.

DEVILED EGGS are a fancy dish for table eating. Remove the shells from 4 hard-boiled eggs; cut in half; remove the yolks and mix them thoroughly with 1 tablespoon of mayonnaise dressing, a pinch of salt, and ½ teaspoon of prepared mustard. A dash of Worcestershire sauce and a teaspoon of vinegar will add the professional touch. Put the resulting paste back into the halves, sprinkle lightly with paprika or celery salt and serve.

AN OMELETTE may be prepared by lightly whipping 3 or 4 eggs, adding 2 tablespoons of melted butter and pouring the batter into a medium-hot, lightly greased frying pan. When nearly cooked, lay grated cheese, bits of cooked ham, fried bacon, tomatoes, or minced cooked onions over one half of the omelette and fold over the other half. Cook a few minutes longer and serve.

FRENCH TOAST is really an egg item, so it enters our calculations right here. Whip up 3 or 4 eggs with a cup of milk; add a teaspoon of salt and 2 tablespoons of sugar. Dip slices of bread in the mixture and fry on a hot, well-greased skillet or frying pan. Usually you resort to this when you have leftover bread, too dry for other use.

Breadstuff

BREAD is a puzzling food item, to the average camper, as the store loaf soon becomes stale and manufacture of a fresh supply appears beyond his skill. There are good substitutes and fill-ins, however.

I find that wheat bread remains palatable for no more than 3 days, in the woods. Rye stays fresh a day or so longer, but usually becomes moldy before it dries out.

The ordinary loaf of baker's bread weighs a pound and cuts up into about 16 slices. Ready-sliced bread is handiest for campers.

PILOT CRACKERS, as vended by the National Biscuit Company, will replace bread to some extent, and remain edible for weeks, if kept dry. They come in 1-pound packages of 12 to 14 pieces, at a gross weight of 1 pound 4½ ounces, and are quite bulky.

SODA CRACKERS are no bargain for the camper, as they soon become stale and soggy in the damp air of the forest. They are fragile, also, and provide nothing more than crumbs after a bit of trail handling.

TRISCUIT is a shredded-wheat wafer which I find very tasty. It may be freshened up, as required, by toasting lightly or warming in an oven. Small packages of Triscuit contain 5 ounces and will amply complement a meal for two men.

RY KRISP is another palatable wafer which remains crisp indefinitely or may be restored to grace by heat. The 7-ounce package contains 4 pieces, 7 × 7½ inches; plenty for 4 individual meals. Smaller and larger packages are available.

BISCUITS are simple enough for anyone, if some such preparation as Bisquick is used. One cup of this ready-mixed flour will provide biscuits for two men, and there are 3 cups in the 1¼-pound package. Follow the instructions on the package and bake in an oven, reflector, or covered pan with heat under and over.

You can bake BISCUIT LOAF in a frying pan. Grease the pan lightly, lay in a thin sheet of dough, hold the pan over the fire to crust the bottom of the loaf and then prop the pan, nearly upright, before the fire.

CORN BREAD may be produced from ready-mixed preparations in much the same manner as biscuits.

ARMY BREAD may be made in a frying pan. Mix 1 cup of flour, 1 tablespoon of sugar, 1 teaspoon of salt and 3 teaspoons of good baking powder; add water to make a thick batter; pour half an inch into a lightly greased pan and proceed as suggested under Biscuit Loaf. Take along the baking powder and flour, if you plan to try this on the trail; I haven't listed them among the pack-sack groceries.

PANCAKES provide breadstuff for breakfasts and may be eaten cold for subsequent meals, as well. You can hardly go wrong with these, if you use one of the better brands of prepared flour. The 1¼-pound packages contain three cups.

One cup of the prepared flour, well-mixed with 1 cup of liquid, will make enough batter to feed two men. Milk provides a richer mixture than water, of course, and if a beaten egg is substituted for part of the liquid, the resulting cakes will benefit greatly. Thin batter makes thin cakes and vice versa, control being accomplished by adding liquid or flour to the batter. Chopped nuts added to the batter will provide a de luxe touch not to be scorned.

To cook pancakes, have your skillet or frying pan hot enough to "bounce back" a drop of water. Grease it lightly, with a bit of raw bacon on a fork or a wad of paper dipped in grease, just before pouring in the batter by spoonfuls. You'll find small cakes easier to manage than large ones and a tablespoon of batter per cake is about right.

Cook each cake until the surface is pitted with bubble holes; turn it gently, with spatula or cake turner, and cook until done — perhaps 5 minutes. A proper pancake should be golden brown on each side, when served.

JOHNNYCAKE: Mix thoroughly 1 cup of yellow corn meal, ½ cup of white flour, 2 tablespoons of sugar, 1 teaspoon of baking powder and a pinch of salt. Add water to form a thick batter, let stand a few minutes while the baking powder gets to work and then drop by spoonfuls into a hot, greased frying pan. A thicker batter may be poured into the pan, as is, and baked, top and bottom, to form a loaf. A quantity of the dry mixture might be prepared at home and carried to camp in a waterproof bag. There is quite a difference in baking powders. You may find more is needed, after your first trial of this recipe.

BOSTON BROWN BREAD and NUT BREAD may be purchased in cans, during normal times, and carried indefinitely. You'll find that one man will readily dispose of a full can of either, without half trying.

DUMPLINGS are dandy as a supplement to stews and may be easily made. Put a cup of Bisquick in a pan, place a tablespoon of butter, bacon grease or other shortening on it and chop into a mixture with knife or spatula. Add about ½ cup of milk to form a thick batter. Drop by spoonfuls into the boiling stew and cook for 12 minutes or so.

Spreads

BUTTER affords a luxurious touch to outdoor meals which can hardly be replaced. It is also highly nourishing and pretty essential to any normal diet. A week's supply may be carried safely in sterilized aluminum cans with screw tops, even in warm weather, but for a long, hard pull you'll need the vacuum-packed article to be obtained from certain vendors. You might write to the Land O' Lakes Creameries,

Inc., Minneapolis 13, Minnesota, and request information
on a ready source. At this moment, I know of no other place
to get it. Don't make the mistake of melting butter into
a can. You will not have butter when you get through.

PEANUT BUTTER is a nourishing dainty which may
be carried for quite a while before rancidity catches up with
it. Try it as a spread on crackers, Ry Krisp, Triscuit or
bread, when you want a between-meals snack.

Sweets

SWEETS are well-nigh essential to outdoor folk and some
provision should be made to satisfy the common craving for
them. Many campers carry candy bars or sweet chocolate for
this purpose, but I lack the will power to ration such stuff
and usually gobble the entire supply in short order. Jam,
marmalade or honey, worked into the meals, serves me
better.

JAM may be purchased in tins containing a pound or so,
but small quantities of MARMALADE and HONEY are
more often found in glass jars, which are fairly heavy. A
pound of honey in glass, for instance, grosses about 22
ounces. There is nothing to prevent its transfer to a lighter
tin, however.

SYRUP may be carried in prepared form, if you wish, but
it is easy enough to make up a supply as needed, from brown
sugar. Put a half cupful into a mixing pan or cup, stir in
just enough water to dissolve it and cook until the solution
is clear. A few drops of maple flavoring might add a taste
you'll like.

Cereals

OATMEAL PORRIDGE: Put ½ cup of rolled oats and
¼ teaspoon of salt in a pot with 1 cup of cold water. Bring
slowly to a boil over a moderate fire, stirring constantly. The

batch will be done when it boils. Chopped dates or raisins, added just before the mush is taken off the fire, will improve it greatly.

CORN MEAL MUSH: Mix ½ cup of corn meal, ½ teaspoon of salt and 1 cup of water in a cooking pot. Bring slowly to a boil over a moderate fire, stirring constantly. Add hot water if the mush gets too thick. Take it off the fire when it begins to boil briskly and let it simmer for 10 minutes or so.

If you like fried corn meal mush, pour the batch into a shallow pan or deep plate and let stand overnight. Slice about ¼ inch thick in the morning, and fry in hot grease until brown. Serve with syrup or honey. Chopped cooked meat, added to the cooked mush, will make it extra special for frying.

BOILED RICE is a fairly tricky item for the amateur cook, as the stuff scorches quite easily. Wash ⅓ cup of rice thoroughly in cold, salted water. Change water and rinse until clear. Bring 1 quart of water to a furious boil, in a fairly large cook pot, and trickle in the rice, a little at a time so as to maintain the boil. Let the pot boil hard, without stirring, until a few grains may be easily crushed against the side with a spoon. Drain off the water as soon after this as you can handle the pot; rinse the rice with cold water, drain, and set it near the fire to swell and dry in moderate heat. You could mix raisins or chopped dates into the cooked rice right after rinsing it, and improve its eating qualities vastly.

Boiled rice may also be mixed with chopped, cooked onions to good effect, and a bit of tomato bouillon added to the mixture wouldn't hurt it a bit.

MACARONI and SPAGHETTI are offered in a variety of combinations, in packages. The manufacturer's directions for cooking are specific and you should have little or no trouble in preparing tasty meals if you follow them. Canned spaghetti is also a fine item for the camp cook who wishes to avoid the puttering required by preparation of raw materials.

Bulk macaroni or the like should be dropped into briskly boiling water with a teaspoon of salt added and cooked about 20 minutes. Rinse it. then, in two or three changes of cold water, and reheat it for serving. A quarter of a pound of macaroni, cooked in 3 pints or more of water, should serve two men generously. After it is cooked and rinsed, it may be put in a pan with a tablespoon of butter and twice as much grated cheese and cooked until the cheese is melted. It should be stirred gently the while. Canned tomatoes cook nicely with it, in the reheating process.

Vegetables

BEANS figure prominently in most dreams of camp cookery, but their possibilities are quite limited, actually. Dried navy beans require a lot of soaking and cooking to make them digestible and the process is a nuisance in any camp lacking a full-time cook. The precooked beans marketed in recent years need comparatively little soaking, but the baking of them requires plenty of oven heat, which is a rare item in a majority of camps. You might try a package, however, and see what you can do with them. Full directions are on the package.

CANNED BEANS are something else again. Eaten cold or hot, they provide quick and tasty meals. Mixed with 2 slices of bacon, diced and fried, and a couple of onions similarly treated, a No. 2 can of even the most mediocre baked beans is something for a pair of hungry campers to anticipate. Get the beans pretty hot, after mixing in the bacon and onion.

If you must have beans and can't afford the weight of

canned goods, give some thought to dried **KIDNEY BEANS**. They may be cooked, without preliminary soaking, in less than 2 hours of simmering and seasoned to taste with butter and salt. Cold, they make dandy salad when mixed with chopped celery and seasoned with vinegar. One cup of dried kidneys, cooked in a quart of water, will amply feed two men.

DRIED SOY BEANS are fine food, but require 3 hours or more of cooking to make them edible, as in the case of navy beans.

POTATOES are pretty essential to any well-balanced outdoor diet. Fresh ones are best, of course, but their weight and bulk often present a considerable problem to the packer. One brand of dehydrated potatoes suits me fine. Jack Gomperts & Company, 24 California Street, San Francisco 11, California, distribute them under the trade name "Dehydrettes" and can supply them in packages of 5 ounces or more, through various agents. The 5-ounce package will provide two meals for two men, thus replacing at least 2 pounds of the fresh article. Thirty minutes of cooking, without preliminary soaking, will prepare the tiny cubes for mashing. Fifteen minutes will get them ready for the frying pan, from whence they emerge as delectable hashed-browns. There may be other brands as good, but I am not familiar with them.

Fresh potatoes require about 30 minutes of boiling, but should be tested with a sliver or fork before graduation to the serving plate. The same applies to baked potatoes, which require about an hour of cooking time.

Mix a bit of raw, chopped onion with mashed potatoes, sometime when you feel fancy.

Cold mashed potatoes make up into tasty cakes, when fried in butter or bacon grease. Mixing them with beaten eggs, before frying, adds to the eating pleasure.

ONIONS, either green or dried, add zest to many camp dishes. Ordinarily the camper will be able to carry only the white, dried kind, which run about 12 to the pound. For 2 portions, peel 4 of these, quarter them and cover with water. Bring them to a boil and they're done. If you like them creamed, add a cup of warmed milk, a tablespoon of butter and season to taste. Cut them in smaller pieces, for frying, or slice them and separate the rings. In stews you may use them in any form. Cooking time is not especially important to the edibility of onions, unless you boil all the goodness out of them. No one will complain if they are served somewhat crisp.

DEHYDRATED ONIONS are more or less of a nuisance to prepare, as they require long soaking before introduction to the fire.

GREEN CABBAGE is highly perishable and will carry well for very few days, but it is a savory food which adds much to camp menus. Served raw, as cole slaw, it requires no more preparation than shredding, washing in cold water and mixing with vinegar. Cooked with ham, or in stews, it should be cut into small pieces and put in the boiling pot about 10 minutes before you expect to eat it. Boiled too long, it will become tough and tasteless. A 1-pound head is ample for two men.

RED CABBAGE also makes good slaw, but requires 20 or 30 minutes of slow cooking.

DEHYDRATED CABBAGE needs to be soaked for hours, before cooking.

SAUERKRAUT is a canned item, so far as the camper is concerned, but it's worth taking if the weight is not too much of a burden. You may eat it raw, as a salad, or cook it with ham, sausage or wieners. Excessive cooking doesn't seem to hurt it much, unless it is scorched. A No. 2 can is enough for a two-man meal.

LETTUCE is a nice item for the first day or two in camp. Eaten with any kind of dressing, or as a garnish for other foods, it is healthful and appetizing. To cook lettuce, perhaps after it wilts a bit, drop into boiling water for just a couple of minutes. A good solid head weighing ½ pound will provide two portions.

GREEN CORN sometimes happens into a camper's life, to brighten a day or two. If you have a pot large enough to accommodate as much as a couple of ears, broken in halves, boil enough water to cover them, stir in a tablespoon of white sugar, drop the corn into the boiling water and cook for 5 or 10 minutes. The corn will be done when you can crush a kernel without squeezing out its milk. Salt it after cooking.

If you have no pot of sufficient size, remove the silk from several ears, twist the husks tight shut, soak them thoroughly in water and bury them shallowly in the hot earth beneath your fire. It will take an hour or more to cook corn in this manner, but the result will be satisfactory.

CANNED CORN comes in two common forms: niblets and cream corn. The first needs only to be thoroughly heated in a pan, with butter, milk and seasoning, and it is ready to eat. The kernels may also be mixed with pancake batter and fried, as fritters. Thick fritters require boiling-hot deep grease; thin ones may be fried in a very hot, well-greased skillet. Serve fritters with syrup or honey.

CREAM CORN is best for mixtures. The contents of a No. 1 can, mixed with 2 eggs and enough crumbs to form a thick batter, will make a batch of corn oysters that could get you the sheriff's job in some counties. Season the mixture with salt and drop onto a very hot, lightly greased griddle or skillet, by spoonfuls. You'll need no syrup or honey with these!

A similar mixture, but thicker, will make into corn pudding. Keep it in the oven until the top is well crusted.

If you must use flour, instead of crumbs, for your batter, add a heaping teaspoon of baking powder to the mix.

CANNED ASPARAGUS may be served cold, in salads. The No. 1 square can is sufficient for this purpose. Salad dressing of any kind will serve to garnish the dish. It is a good side dish when heated and served with butter.

WATER CRESS may be found in many streams and used as essential green stuff. You may cook it, if you wish, and will find it somewhat similar to spinach.

CANNED VEGETABLES such as tomatoes, string beans, beets, peas, carrots, are fine items for camp fare and easily prepared. About all they need is thorough heating and seasoning. No. 1 cans are about right for two people.

Never attempt to heat canned goods in the container unless a hole is punched in the top end for escape of steam. Otherwise, you run some chance of a messy explosion.

If an opened can is heated in boiling water, take care to prevent dilution of the contents. The opening should be kept above the water level in the heating vessel.

Beverages

COFFEE: Use the coarse-ground article and allow 1 heaping tablespoon for each big cup. Put the coffee and the required amount of water in the pot, stir into a mixture and heat until the water starts to bubble. Take it off the fire then, and allow it to steep for 5 minutes. Another method is to bring the water to a boil, pour a little into a cup, with the coffee, stir it up and add the mixture to the pot of boiling water as you take it off the fire. Let the brew steep for 10 minutes, in this instance.

In either case, a dash of cold water, down the spout of the pot, will settle the grounds. Some folks believe a pinch of salt added to the dry coffee improves the brew, but I can take it or leave it.

CONCENTRATED COFFEE makes a good brew in the easiest possible manner, but lacks something in taste, after a few days' use. It is very convenient, however, and well worth consideration. A 4-ounce package of the stuff will make approximately 30 cups of beverage; just about the amount provided by a pound of ground coffee.

INSTANT POSTUM is a pretty good substitute for coffee and very easily prepared.

TEA is best made in the cup, using a tea ball and pouring boiling water over it. Individual tea balls run 100 to the half pound.

COCOA preparations vary somewhat and directions on the package should be followed. Before you try any particular brand, make sure the directions require nothing you'll be without in camp.

MILK is available in two forms, so far as the camper is concerned: evaporated and powdered. Nearly everyone is familiar with evaporated milk and has an established prejudice for or against it. If you plan to use it on cereal, without previous experience, make an experiment at home, to determine how much, if any, you'll need for each meal. It is heavy stuff to carry, in any quantity.

The tall cans of evaporated milk contain 14½ ounces (by weight) and gross 17 ounces. Small cans contain 6 ounces (by weight) and gross 7 ounces.

If you will open milk tins by piercing a small pouring hole on one side, just below the top rim, and an air vent in the same position on the opposite side, both openings may be closed with a large rubber band or a strip of adhesive tape. Thus you may carry the partially used contents without much danger of spilling. It is much easier, of course, to jab two holes in the top of the can and hope to plug them for transit, but the plugs will usually work loose if not secured with tape or rubber band.

POWDERED MILK requires quite a bit of mixing with water, to produce a palatable beverage, but most people prefer it to evaporated milk, for use on cereals. You'll need a fairly deep vessel, such as a cook pot, to mix it properly, as it must be whipped very briskly with a fork or egg-beater. KLIM is the best brand I know of and full directions are on each can. The cans come in various sizes, but are none too handy to carry, after being opened. The covers fall off easily. Probably a screw-top aluminum butter can should be provided for transport of the loose supply.

Synthetic milk, such as CAROLENE, affords the advantage of being easy to whip, for fancy desserts, and such. It comes in cans similar to those containing evaporated milk.

Salads

SALADS help greatly to relieve the monotony of camp meals and are easy to prepare when kitchen facilities are at hand. Fruits — fresh, cooked or dried — may be mixed with nuts and celery, to make tasty salads. Nearly all raw vegetables, except potatoes, combine to good effect. Mayonnaise or French dressing will lend flavor to either fruit or vegetable salads, but vinegar is relished by most people on vegetables only. Salmon or tuna fish may be mixed with chopped onions and celery, as it comes out of the can, and made to serve as the base of an entire meal.

Try this one, some hot night when the cook stove has no appeal.

Supper Salad

Making use of leftover vegetables:

1 cup cooked kidney or Lima beans — drained
1 cup cooked peas — drained
1 small onion diced finely
½ cup diced celery or ½ teaspoon celery salt
½ cup or more of diced cheese
Enough mayonnaise to hold salad together — mixed lightly with fork to avoid mashing vegetables
2 hard-boiled eggs cut in large pieces — added as a garnish

Desserts

DESSERTS are simple enough. Prepared pudding mixes are sold in small packages bearing full directions for use and require no more preparation than mixing with milk and brief cooking. The chocolate items are especially good when nut meats are added. Heinz offers plum, fig and date puddings in small cans just right for two diners. You may heat them in the can, with about 20 minutes of boiling, and serve with hard sauce made of butter and sugar.

There are all kinds of canned fruit, as you know, but it is difficult to find anything other than fruit salad in very small cans. Leftover fruit and juice are awkward to transport, as you can imagine, and a No. 1 can of fruit is usually more than enough for a twosome meal. In permanent quarters, a good scheme is to eat part of a No. 2 can for supper dessert and carry over the balance, for breakfast.

Any of the canned fruits will top off a split biscuit, to afford a version of shortcake.

PACKAGED COOKIES may be carried successfully for quite a while, if reasonable care is exercised to keep them dry.

GINGERBREAD may be produced from prepared mixtures when oven facilities are at hand. Follow directions on the package.

Dried Fruits

Apricots, prunes, figs, dates and raisins I reckon as diet essentials and for that reason do not list them as desserts. You should eat some of one or the other every day, while in the woods, for the good of your soul and the benefit of your bowels.

DRIED APRICOTS usually run about 48 to the pound; enough for 6 or 8 portions. Unless directions on the pack-

age state otherwise, they require thorough washing in cold
water, a start in hot water to cover and about 40 minutes
of simmering. You may want to add sugar, to sweeten them.
The tenderized brands generally require less cooking.

DRIED PRUNES may also be figured for 6 or 8 portions
per pound. They require the same preparation as apricots
and about an hour of simmering. Part of a lemon, sliced
into a batch of cooking prunes, vastly improves the flavor,
or a few drops of lemon extract will do nearly as well.
Sugar may be added while cooking, if you think it is needed.
If you buy tenderized or other packaged fruit, read the
directions on the package — they may differ from mine.

You'll find it most handy to cook apricots and prunes in
the evening, when time is not at a premium. Carry-overs,
for breakfast, are best guarded in screw-top cans or jars,
when out of doors.

RAISINS, DATES and FIGS may be eaten as they come
out of the package, or chopped and added to cereals in the
last few minutes of cooking.

Preparation of Fish and Game

Having delved into the mysteries of grocery store and
butcher shop victuals, let us now explore the possibilities
of fish and game.

A desperately hungry man will find some food value in
nearly any creature he can bring to bag from aquatic or
sylvan haunts, the principal exception being a few tropical
fish which are poisonous. There are degrees of palatability
in wild flesh, however, and I shall deal only with such
quarry as affords the prospect of good eating, without attempting to cover the full range of edible wild life. Several

items of common knowledge will be treated and you may go on from there, if experimentation appeals to you, or is forced upon you.

Fish

Any fish will depreciate in food value if treated as rubbish between the time of taking and the moment of serving. How often do you see a fisherman dump a mess of stiff and withered trout from his creel, or retrieve several sun-dried bass from the filthy bottom of a boat? Too often — and only because of careless disregard for decent handling. Trout should be killed, with a sharp rap on the head from knife handle, priest or stick, before going into the creel. If it is impracticable to wrap the fish in waxed or parchment paper, as creeled, green leaves or grass should be placed around them, to retain moisture and preserve freshness. Damp cloth or paper will serve the same purpose.

Heavier fish deserve similar treatment. Unless you can keep them alive, on a stringer or in a live box, kill them when caught and at least keep them out of the sun and dirt.

Certainly, you should clean fish before putting them under refrigeration and refrain from laying them directly on ice, where they will absorb too much moisture.

Frozen fish should be thawed in very cold water before cooking.

It is not good practice to wash fish before frying, as the wet flesh will absorb excessive grease. It is better to wipe them clean with a clean cloth or absorbent paper.

SMALL TROUT require no scaling or skinning and are easily cleaned. Cut off the head, just back of the forward fins; slit the belly from the vent forward and clean out the cavity. Run your thumbnail or the back of a knife blade up the backbone, to remove the blood, and wipe clean, inside and out.

Cut through the backbone in one or two places to prevent

curling, and fry in plenty of very hot grease or oil until nice and brown. Keep your grease hot by dropping in only one fish at a time. Season with salt and pepper as the skin begins to brown. Rolling trout in corn meal or flour, before frying, detracts from the flavor. Save that technique for bass or pike.

Any small fish, such as trout, may be cooked over a bed of coals, without utensils, by skewering several on a stiff stick of green wood, with thin strips of bacon or fat pork between them. Turn the stick constantly as it is held over the coals, so that the melting fat will baste the fish and not drop into the fire.

PAN FISH, other than trout, require scaling or skinning, and for my money the skinning process is best on all counts. Cut deep on either side of the top fins and remove them by catching the rear end between the knife edge and thumb and pulling up, toward the head. Then cut through the skin — up the back, from head to tail, and back of the forward fin, on either side, from spine to belly. Cut off the tail, or cut through the skin in front of it, on either side. Hold the fish by the head; loosen a generous corner of skin at the backbone, back of the head; catch it firmly between knife and thumb and rip off the entire side. Turn the fish and skin the other side in similar manner. A slash of the knife along the belly will complete the skinning and serve to remove entrails. Cut off the head as a final operation.

I like to fillet all fish but small trout, if they are to be broiled or fried. This is accomplished by using the framework of the fish as a guide for the flat of your knife. Insert the blade, edge toward tail, at the head end of the backbone. Keeping the blade as close to the bone as possible, cut back toward the tail, about an inch deep. Fold back the flesh, as you repeat this cut several times, and the eventual reward will be a fine solid fillet of fish, free of bones. Such fillets will fry or broil very quickly. You will probably botch your first attempt at filleting and wind up with broken pieces of fish, which will taste just as good, however, for all their ragged appearance. Brief experience will make you an expert, no doubt.

Skinned fillets of BASS, PIKE and PICKEREL have none of the "muddy" taste sometimes noticed in these fish. BULLHEADS and CATFISH respond to the same treatment, but somewhat stubbornly, because of their slipperiness. Watch out for their spines, in forward and top fins! They can give you a painful wound.

If you possess a reflector oven, you may enjoy roasted fish. Rub the dressed carcass, or fillets, lightly with butter or bacon grease; place in the pan; dab in a few half-teaspoons of butter or grease, here and there; and cook in front of a good fire, as you would bake biscuits. The fish will be done when it is brown on top.

A baking pan similarly filled with fish will produce good results in a stove oven, if you are careful not to dry out the fish by overcooking.

Very large fish may be cut into steaks, for convenience in cooking. Roast these as suggested, or broil them on a lightly greased griddle over a moderate fire.

EELS may be skinned and filleted in the same manner as that prescribed for fish. The flesh is too oily for successful frying, but may be rolled in meal and broiled, with good results.

Frog Legs

Frogs, both big and little, provide a tasty supplement to camp fare which is well worth looking into.

A majority of camp cooks prepare only the legs of frogs, but in some sections of the country the back meat of a bullfrog is considered a delicacy of equal merit.

In any event, skin the portion you decide to use and soak

for an hour in cold water, to which vinegar or salt has been added. Two tablespoons of either vinegar or salt to a quart of water should be about right. After soaking, wipe dry; roll in flour seasoned lightly with salt and pepper and fry slowly in butter or other shortening until a nice brown crust encases the meat.

Game

Most game affords better eating than the average hunter suspects. Better than he deserves, in fact, unless each carcass is treated with decent consideration for cleanliness and edibility.

I find no merit in the general practice of keeping game for hours, and sometimes days, before cleaning. The contents of intestines will certainly commence to sour shortly after natural processes are stopped by death, and it seems senseless to risk the spoilage of good meat by failure to remove them. Acquire the habit of cleaning your game as you kill it. The task will be easier when the carcass is still warm, and your reward will be finer food when the meat reaches the table. Carry a modest supply of cheesecloth or waxed paper with you when hunting small game, and wrap your kill after dressing it, for the sake of cleanliness.

The flesh of any warm-blooded creature is not fit to eat until it has cooled thoroughly. More often than not it will sicken you if eaten too soon, and in any event will be tough and tasteless. Let your game hang for at least two days, well protected from bugs and dirt, before you cook it.

Liver may be excepted from this rule and cooked as soon as you please. The sooner the better, in fact, as it is quite perishable. In all animals except those of the deer family, and in all fowls except pheasant, a comparatively small, dark-greenish sac will be found attached to the liver, usually near the center. This is the gall bladder, containing an extremely bitter fluid certain to spoil any meat it touches. Remove it very carefully, sacrificing a fairly generous portion of the liver adjacent to the point of attachment for the sake of safety.

If the liver has been taken from an old animal, it should be parboiled before frying. Place it in a pot with sufficient water to cover; simmer gently for about half an hour; skim off such scum as arises to the surface; fish it out and wipe it dry. Cut the parboiled liver into slices and fry in a hot skillet, well greased. Sliced or chopped onions may be added, if your skillet is large enough, and fried with the liver.

Some cooks skin liver before cooking. Others dredge it with seasoned flour, brown it quickly on both sides, add a little water and let it simmer in a covered skillet for 20 or 25 minutes.

Many hunters spit deer liver on a green stick, together with a bit of fat, and roast it over an open fire, with no thought of parboiling, soaking or other preparation.

RABBIT has fallen into some disrepute as table game, because of the wide publicity given tularemia, or "rabbit fever." The fact is, however, that diseased animals are comparatively rare, and if sick-looking or weak-acting rabbits are avoided, little danger will be incurred. The peppy rabbit is usually healthy. Tularemia may be contracted by humans, through cuts or abrasions on the hands, while handling infected animals, so it is a wise precaution to wear rubber gloves when dressing rabbits. The skin and viscera should be burned, to eliminate the possibility of foraging dogs being infected. If you discover white spots on the liver of a rabbit, you may be quite certain of the presence of tularemia, but cooking will destroy the bacteria and render the flesh safe for eating. The warty growths sometimes found on the skins of cottontail rabbits do not indicate disease and you may ignore them.

Clean your rabbit by slitting the skin of his belly with a sharp knife. Avoid ripping through the intestines, which will make a messy and unsanitary job of the cleaning. Once the abdominal cavity is open, you may take a backhanded grip on fore and hind legs and, with a snappy slinging motion, downward and away from you, remove all the entrails in one operation. If the carcass is still warm, you can skin it by tearing the skin on the back of the neck and peeling it off clear to the feet. Needless to say, you will use your knife to remove head, feet and tail. Look for a waxy gland under each front leg, right up where it joins the body, and cut it out.

After the dressed rabbit has hung for at least 24 hours in cool weather, or longer if the temperature is fairly high, cut the carcass into 6 or 8 pieces, wipe them dry and simmer in enough water to cover for about 10 minutes. Skim off such scum as may appear. A spoonful of vinegar or lemon juice in the water is desirable, if you have it, or an onion will serve just as well, to add a bit of flavor.

For fried rabbit, drain these parboiled pieces; roll them in flour and fry on both sides until brown, in a very hot pan, lightly greased.

You may roast disjointed rabbit in a folding reflector oven by laying a strip of raw bacon over each piece and basting frequently with the grease that trickles out into the pan. The meat will be done when it is brown on top.

Stewed rabbit is prepared by simmering the cut-up carcass until tender — which takes from one to two hours, depending on the critter's condition and size. This is a continuation of the parboiling process previously mentioned and you should be careful to avoid hard boiling, which will toughen the meat. Put in an onion or two after the meat becomes tender, and give some thought to adding dumplings.

SQUIRRELS are prepared for the table in much the same manner as rabbits. An old, tough squirrel may require as much as half an hour of parboiling (gentle simmering in water) before frying, but young ones are often fried or fricasseed without such preliminary cooking.

To fricassee a squirrel, season each piece of the cut-up carcass with salt and pepper; roll in flour and fry in a pan with chopped-up bacon for about 30 minutes, or until well browned. (Two slices of bacon should be enough for each squirrel.) Then add chopped onion and enough water to half cover the meat; cover the pan and cook slowly for nearly 3 hours.

Game Birds

Game birds are not so very different from domestic fowl, so far as preparation and cooking are concerned. Their meat is dryer, as a general rule, and usually benefits from the addition of fat in the form of butter or bacon grease.

The practice of skinning game birds, rather than plucking them, appears to be gaining in popularity. Some hunters believe part of the flavor is lost in this manner, but I haven't noticed any difference important enough to worry about.

The principles of skinning a bird are about the same as those applying to small animals. Cut off the head; slit the skin up the belly, from vent to neck; peel it down the back and over the wings as far as possible; cut off the last joints on the wings; continue peeling down the back and over the legs until you have to cut off the feet.

It might be well to mention, right here, that game birds should not be skinned, or plucked, until safely in the kitchen and ready for the cook. Loss of feathers is loss of identity in the bird department and conservation officers are sometimes very narrow-minded about it.

Anyhow, skin your bird or pluck him dry, as you see fit, and, in the case of waterfowl, remove the oil sac from the vicinity of the tail. Wipe out the emptied abdominal cavity with a clean dry cloth and make up your mind on the mode of cooking.

If you intend to fry, cut the bird into 6 or 8 pieces; simmer these, gently, in enough water to cover, until tender; then remove and drain. Roll the pieces in flour seasoned with salt and pepper and fry in a hot, well-greased pan until crispy and brown on the outside.

To roast a partridge, prairie chicken or pheasant, leave the bird whole, after dressing. Rub a little salt on the outside and lay in the roasting pan, back down. Fasten 2 or 3 strips of bacon across the breast and roast in an oven or reflector for about 40 minutes. Baste the bird, from time to time, with such juice as accumulates in the pan. You could chop up celery and onions, if available, and place them in the cavity before cooking.

Wild duck is roasted in the same manner, but usually requires no bacon. Roast duck suits most people best when slightly rare, and 20 to 30 minutes of roasting, per pound of duck, in a moderate oven, will serve the purpose. You may fill the duck with sliced apples and sew the cavity shut before cooking, if you wish, but I prefer the natural flavor. Fancy cooks sometimes baste roasting duck with orange juice.

Large birds, such as turkeys and geese, present quite a problem to camp cooks with limited facilities, but there is nothing to prevent the frying or roasting of slices from the carcass.

A fairly large wild goose will roast in a moderate oven in about 2 hours. Prepare as suggested for ducks.

A large turkey requires close to 3 hours of roasting in a moderate oven (375° F.).

Venison

Venison, no doubt, suffers more from amateur butchering than any other game. Perhaps the excitement of downing such noble quarry causes some hunters to lose their common sense, but whatever the reason, a lot of scandalous abuse is visited upon dead deer.

Let us hope that your deer has died quickly and painlessly, from a well-placed shot, so that the fever of protracted pain will not have affected his flesh. Drag the carcass into position where you can work on it, with rump lower than the rest of the body, and get about the dressing immediately.

Roll the deer on his back and spread the hind legs. Tie one to a tree or bush, if you can't keep it out of the way in any other manner.

Cut out the genitals. Cut around the anus, so that later it will come free with the intestines. Insert the point of your knife in the hide, as far down on the belly as practicable, and slit the hide only clear to the breast bone, being very careful not to puncture the paunch. This is most easily done with a small blade, holding it edge up on the first two fingers and steadied by the thumb. Thus the two fingers serve as a guide, while the back of the hand presses down the intestines.

Peel back the hide from the belly and cut through the thin wall of muscles which hold the intestines in place. Again be careful not to puncture the paunch. With the intestines exposed, reach into the chest cavity with your knife and cut off the windpipe and large arteries ahead of the lungs. You should now be able to roll out the lungs, liver, heart, paunch and intestines with a little assistance from one hand and perhaps a cut or two with the knife blade where severance from the body is incomplete.

Clean out all remaining scraps of lung and intestine from the cavity, and remove any foreign matter which may be present.

Pick up the liver for camp meat, and if you have nothing to wrap it in, place it in the cavity for transport back to camp.

A deer hunter should be equipped with 15 or 20 feet of stout clothesline or small Manila rope, to aid in getting his game out of the woods. The best method, for short distances, is to drag the animal on his back, head foremost. Tie the forelegs to the head, before starting. Back-packing a deer carcass is fairly dangerous business, in heavily hunted territory. Some fool may be attracted by the antlers or color of the hide and pitch a few shots at what he thinks is a fair target.

A bush or small tree serves nicely as a sled on which to drag out a deer.

Hang your deer, head up, when you get him into camp, and prop open the cavity with a stick 8 or 10 inches long, sharpened on both ends. Wipe the cavity with a clean, dry cloth. Open the vent for drainage, and protect the raw flesh from bugs if there are any about.

Now you are well on the way toward a winter supply of good venison. If you can, get the carcass into cold storage or a deep-freeze locker at the earliest possible moment. Otherwise, have your butcher cut up the carcass and store the cuts until you are ready to use them. Venison improves under cold storage just as beef does.

You'll find that professional butchering pays dividends in good meat. An amateur usually spoils as much as he saves and rarely gets the cuts into the best form for proper cooking.

Young and tender venison affords fine roasts, steaks and chops. As a general rule, loins, rounds, shoulders and rumps provide the best roasts, in the order listed; loins and rounds are the source of steaks and chops are cut from the ribs. Neck, shanks, breasts and flanks serve best for stews and ground meat offerings.

To roast young venison, trim most of the fat from the meat; rub lightly with salt and pepper; place in an uncovered pan, fat side up, and lay 6 or 8 strips of raw bacon over the top. Add no water. Roast slowly in an oven no hotter than 350° F., allowing about 25 minutes of cooking, per pound of meat.

Old or tough venison will not dry-roast too successfully and should be considered first for pot roasts. Trim off as much fat as possible; sprinkle liberally with flour, seasoned with salt and pepper; brown on all sides, in a very hot, well-greased pan; place in a pot with about 1 cup of water; cover tightly and cook very slowly, over the fire, for 2 or 3 hours. Turn the roast occasionally and when it is tender add onions, potatoes, carrots and celery in the quantity desired. Cook until the vegetables are done. Stir flour into the juice left in the pan, for gravy.

Tender steaks and chops from young venison may be broiled or fried. Try the broiling over glowing coals, in the event you have no broiling oven. Simply brown on the fire side; turn and repeat the process. For each side 8 or 10 minutes of cooking is required. Season after cooking.

Steaks and chops should be fried in a very hot pan, lightly greased with butter or bacon fat. Get the pan good and hot before putting in the meat; cook one side about 8 minutes; turn and cook the other side the same. Season after cooking.

Tough venison steaks are best prepared in the same manner as pot roasts. Rub both sides with flour, seasoned with salt and pepper. Brown both sides quickly in a very hot frying pan, well greased. Then add half a cup of water; cover the pan and cook slowly, over the fire, until tender. When tender (after about 1 hour of cooking) add onions, celery and a cup of canned tomatoes. Cook until the vegetables are done.

Venison unsuitable for roasting, broiling or frying should be stewed or ground. To stew, cut the meat into small pieces; sprinkle with seasoned flour; brown quickly in hot grease; cover with boiling water and simmer gently in a covered pot until tender. Vegetables and dumpling dough may be added, then, and the cooking continued until they are done.

Ground venison may be cooked in the same manner as chopped steak or hamburger.

Good Camp Cookery

The essentials of good camp cookery may be summarized about as follows — not necessarily in order of importance:

Clean and convenient utensils.
Steady heat.
Quality groceries.
Careful measurements.
Thorough preparation.
Scheduling, with regard to slow- and rapid-cooking items.
Consistent attention.
Frequent testing.
Notes for future reference.

Bear in mind that:
Different brands of foodstuffs may vary in characteristics.
Cooking is slower in high altitudes.
Water varies greatly in mineral content and flavor.
It is better to use too little, rather than too much, seasoning.

INDEX